To Win, Build, and Send

Preparing to Live a Truly Great Life in Christ

—ᴡ—

By Bobby D. Hopper

Forward by Pastor Robert G. Newlin

Endorsements

—ɯɯ—

"I have the privilege of listening to Pastor Bobby every Sunday. The Lord has gifted this humble man with the ability to reach the heart of a listener. In this book, as in church, I feel as though Pastor Bobby is speaking directly to me. His message often fills my eyes with tears as I relate it to my life in Christ. Pastor Bobby illustrates a powerful story about when his son was near death in the hospital. He felt angry and alone, and he actually yelled at God, asking, "Why my boy?" God replied, "He's not yours." When I think about the beautiful faces of my own children, I imagine what it would have been like to be told, "They're not yours." In the book, Pastor Bobby goes on to discover God had a plan for his family that day. The book is full of stories that tug at my heart; others encourage me to move beyond my own fears and trust the Lord is guiding me to do His work. I am reminded of my Christian obligation to use the gifts I was given. Without question, this book made it clear that in order to build a strong foundation, I must study God's Word; only then will I be able to educate others. I am fortunate to call Bobby Hopper my friend and blessed to be guided by him to a deeper understanding of my faith."

—Landi Halloran, M.D., Internal Medicine/Pediatrics

"Pastor Bobby Hopper's vision in *Win, Build, and Send* is not just another formula to grow your church's numbers. It is a challenge to each of us to grow in our personal relationship with Jesus Christ. It will be by the personal desire of each church member to win, build, and send in Jesus' name that our churches will fulfill the Great Commission from Matthew 28. We need to take the challenge in this book seriously."

—Mark Scott, Elder, Fillmore Christian Church

"There are no 'secret keys,' 'mysteries revealed,' or 'spiritual breakthroughs,' so popular today in evangelical books, in *Win, Build, and Send*. Pastor Hopper has simply offered practical tips for any believer who truly wants to live out the Great Commission. Readers will be touched by his heartwarming (and sometimes heart*breaking*) stories from the front lines of Christian ministry today. The author's passion for Christ is evident in *Win, Build, and Send*, which was born of a true servant's heart. It was refreshing to read the work of an author who actually lives out what he writes."

—Oscar Lynch, Author, *Wheat From Chaff:*
A Guide to Today's Popular Movements

Table of Contents

—⟋⟍—

Acknowledgments

—⟶⟶—

I want to thank God my Father for His guidance, inspiration, grace, and mercy as I have traveled this road.

I want to thank my wife, Cami, for her faith in my gifts and abilities. I want to thank her for understanding when I was not an understanding person.

I want to tell my two beautiful children, Tyler and Lauren, that I love them, and I pray that this book and my life will assist them in their relationship with Christ.

I want to thank my parents, George and Joann, for their prayers and support throughout my entire life.

I want to thank Arlo and Karen, my in-laws, for their constant prayers and belief in me.

I want to thank Becki Arnold for her wonderful talents and prayers for the back cover of this book..

I want to thank my friend Bob. You are a true friend in every biblical aspect of the word.

I want to thank Oscar, Mark, and Landi for their support and feedback.

I want to thank my wonderful, loving church family at Fillmore Christian Church. You live the true essence of winning, building, and sending for His kingdom and have supported my family and made us your family.

I want to thank you, the reader, for trusting enough to read this book. I pray it will bless your life.

In Christ,

Bobby D. Hopper

Foreword

By Pastor Robert G. Newlin

—◊◊◊—

It has been my observation and experience that we as a culture struggle with evangelism and discipleship within the church and our own lives. We have conveniently separated these two aspects of ministry to fit our own agendas, and we also have minimized our potential and witness as "disciple-makers." Evangelism and discipleship are not only spiritual gifts one might possess, but more importantly are our God-given responsibilities as Christians. I believe these two aspects of a disciple are not only inseparable, but also equally important in our journey as we "live life to the fullest" here on this earth.

It is not a coincidence or a surprise that my dear friend and accountability partner of the past three years has decided to share this passion of his with us all. From the beginning of his ministry in our community, he has planted this seed and vision "for living" as the vision for his congregation, as well as how to live one's life. The concept of win, build, and send, therefore, is not just a motto for Bobby and his Christian walk, but a conviction, commitment, and passion that he lives daily.

Bobby has taken the gospel message and broken it down into its simplest form to help us draw closer to a Savior Who desires us to develop and live out the philosophy of win, build, and send. Bobby has truly taken this philosophy of life and ministry and made it work for him in a powerful and special way. I have marveled at how Bobby has been able to experience some difficult and life-changing personal adventures, yet achieve a balance of love and grace within his life and ministry. Bobby is encouraging each of us through this book to become more than just an evangelist or a disciple, but one who wants to make a difference in our own life AND those around us!

I believe you will find this book is a valuable resource if you desire to make a difference in your life and in the lives of others. I can only pray this book will impact you as much as Bobby has made a lasting impression upon me to "live life to the fullest." I believe this book Bobby has written, our friendship, and our Savior Jesus Christ's desire for us to "live" can be summed up in Paul's greeting to the Philippians: "I thank my God every time I remember you. In all my prayers for all of you, I always pray with joy because of your partnership in the gospel from the first day until now, being confident of this, that he who began a good work in you will carry it on to completion until the day of Christ Jesus" (Philippians 1:3-6, NIV).

INTRODUCTION

What Is Win, Build, and Send?

—⟋w⟍—

Then Jesus came to them and said, "All authority in heaven and on earth has been given to me. Therefore go and make disciples of all nations, baptizing them in the name of the Father and of the Son and of the Holy Spirit, and teaching them to obey everything I have commanded you. And surely I am with you always, to the very end of the age."

Matthew 28:18-20

To understand what Win, Build, and Send is, we need to start at the beginning. The beginning is the very start of a person's life. No, I am not speaking of your physical birth; I am speaking of when you truly start to live. Some will say this begins when the kids grow up and move out of the home. Others say it starts when they find true financial freedom. I have heard it said that life begins when we allow ourselves to really begin to live.

I believe that physical life begins upon conception. As a matter of fact, I recently did a funeral service for a small infant. The child died while still in the mother's womb, a very young mother's womb.

You will get very different opinions about when life truly begins. Some say at three weeks the heart begins to beat, while others say life does not begin until birth. I have a little different view about life stages; thus the theory of win, build, and send.

In 1998, I was inspired by the thought to win people to Christ, build a foundation of truth in them, and send them out prepared to win others to Christ. I found this a very simple thought for implementing the gospel. However, I discovered I could not do this until I had experienced and applied it to my own life. I began to really search my life from the core. I found I did not like who I had become. Oh, I was doing great in the eyes of my peers. I was a successful youth pastor, coach, and athletic director for a wonderful church and school. I was respected by my peers and on my way to a wonderful career. Although life was going very well, there was still something very incomplete in my life. I had not even really begun to live. I made my mind up that from that moment forward, I would apply the principles you will read about in this book.

This book is not intended to be a large, complicated, deep theology type of book. This book is meant to assist you on a great life in Christ. The book was written in a simple style. It was written to be direct, applicable, and encouraging.

I pray this book will bring to you a fresh perspective on the Christian life and hopefully encourage you to really live life to its fullest. Win, build, and send is a unique way of looking at life through the eyes of Christ. We will go on a journey together to enrich your life and prayerfully the lives of many others with whom you come into contact.

As you read this book, I would encourage you to stop along the way and examine where you are on your road in life. Examine your daily comings and goings, your work time and play times, your finances and givings, and your talents and passions. I want you to truly live and to live life to its fullest.

God has pressed upon my heart the win, build, and send concept for the past several years. I have been convinced that this vision can help every Christian with their daily walk. I believe it can direct every church with fulfilling the vision that it may have.

My prayer for you is that you will be moved, touched, and encouraged to truly win in this life because of what God can and will do in and through you.

Know that I, the author, am praying for you, the reader. In fact, I want to do something different than most authors. I want to challenge you to read this book and as you go through it to reflect and keep notes. When you have finished this book, contact me and give me your thoughts, stories, and experiences.

If this book encourages you, then pass it on to someone else and encourage him or her to do the same. To win, build, and send is more than a simple concept. Win, build, and send are a vision. Every person needs a vision to succeed. I have included a Study Guide in the back of the book. Each lesson corresponds with a chapter. This is an additional tool to help you go deeper in your experience with Win, Build, and Send. I encourage you to do this as an individual, while you read this book, or as a group in a study setting.

By applying the concept of the win, build, and send method, you can live the Christian life to its fullest and experience all God has in store for you. We are told in Hosea 4:14, "A people without understanding will come to ruin!" We need a clear understanding, a vision, of what we are to do with our Christianity. I pray this small book can lead you in your understanding of how to win, build, and send for the kingdom of Christ!

May God bless your journey as you win, build, and send for His kingdom.

CHAPTER 1

To Win

—⚡—

Therefore go and make disciples of all nations,
baptizing them in the name of the Father and of the
Son and of the Holy Spirit.

Matthew 28:19

I am a guy who loves sports. I grew up in Texas, where
football was king. I played football, watched football, and
even dreamed about football. It was the way of life for a kid
in the heart of Texas. I dreamed big dreams as I watched the
Houston Oilers play in the Astrodome. I would play in the
front yard and fantasize that I was Johnnie Unitas or Roger
Staubach. I ended every fantasy with time running out and
me throwing the winning touchdown as time expired. I won
the Superbowl! What a wonderful life that would have been.

I am a very competitive person. I love to win. I love to
win debates, athletic endeavors, and just about anything
anyone wants to dive into. I love to see competition. I enjoy
seeing the underdog win. I like a good thumping. I like to
win! I was a very competitive teen and young adult. I wanted
to be on top of the world, but only through the eyes of the
world. Life has a way of humbling us.

I thought I would be a professional athlete all my life, or a preacher of a church of several thousand people. I wanted to win by the world standards. No matter what my heart said, I wanted to gauge myself by what the world labeled as success.

Years later, I find myself in small-town America as a small-town preacher, and I am not throwing touchdowns. I am not a professional athlete, and I do not have a church of several thousand people. Life takes a lot of twists, but we were made to win this game of life. My fantasies have changed, and so have my passions and desires. When we allow our lives to be led by the Authority of the universe, we start to see victory in a different light. We start to see life in a way the world cannot comprehend. We start to see others as more important than we had thought. We begin to see others as more important than ourselves. Life will take on a completely new meaning when we allow God to actually take the lead.

We were made to excel in life. We were designed for greatness. We have this calling from the pit of our stomachs that there must be more to life than just living and dying. The problem with most of us is that we chase the wrong goals, desires, or even fantasies. How can we expect to excel in life when life tells us that it is okay to quit? It seems so prevalent in our society to just quit when things get tough. We tell our children to quit piano, sports, or even educational endeavors if they are too difficult or no longer enjoyable. We lay a foundation for them to be able to quit other things as they grow older. We quit our jobs when we feel mistreated. We quit our marriages when we cannot find the answers we are looking for. Some of our loved ones have even decided to quit life.

We chase goals that the world has set, that have no true reward. We work hard to get ahead, only to be passed by. We study to pass the test, only to fail. We labor in our marriages, only for our marriage to end in divorce or discontent. We work so hard in life to achieve and the world keeps knocking us down. How do we become triumphant in a world that is such an overwhelming opponent?

Even when we succeed in the world's view, the reward we receive is only with the values and rewards the world can offer us. If we get the promotion, we receive monetary gain, power, and accolades. We pass a test, only to prepare for another and possibly receive a degree. I think you get the point. These rewards are not bad, but these rewards should not be the main prize of what we are pursuing. These worldly rewards are only temporary and will fade away with time. We will spend the money, get used to the promotion, and find ourselves still lacking in the desire of accomplishment. No matter what the world can give us, we will eventually find ourselves looking for more.

Notice a child with a new toy. The child may have wanted this toy for a long time, but after a while, the child will discard the toy. It may become broken or just simply lose its appeal. Whatever the case, the child will eventually want something new to replace the joy the toy once brought. We are not much different from that child. The main difference is simply the object of our affection. We must break this cycle and change what rewards we are pursuing, or we will never experience true victory upon this earth.

I am here to tell you that you can win in this life if you set your mind to the proper perspective. I am not speaking of the "power of positive thinking." I am not talking about cheating to get ahead. I am talking about truly winning against this thing called life, tasting the wonderful flavor of victory each day. How? you may ask.

Let us look at the lives of some people who won against insurmountable odds to get a proper understanding of winning.

Joseph the "Winner"

Genesis 37:5 says, "Joseph had a dream."

Joseph of the Bible was a person who had big dreams in life. Joseph dreamed that he would have a very high position and that even his own siblings and parents would be subjective to him and his decisions. Their very life would fall into his hands if so. Now, Joseph had grand dreams of winning in life, but it was not without some severe roadblocks.

At the tender age of seventeen, he was sold into slavery by the very family members he would rule in his dreams. Later, after overcoming great odds, Joseph became a very powerful man in his country, but after a false allegation, he was thrown into jail and stripped of his position. Now, Joseph could have given up while he was in prison, but instead he was given great authority in the prison system. Once released from prison, in about a fifteen-minute period of time, he went from prisoner to second in command of an entire country.

I know this sounds a little unrealistic, but what drove Joseph was not a dream of life, but a true view of living an excellent life. Joseph had set his life apart for honoring God in all circumstances. He chose to live life to its fullest no matter where he lived it. Whether it would be in slavery, jail, or in the command of a country, Joseph did not change his way of living due to his circumstances. We can take so much from his story, for we are a society that changes with the latest fad or idea.

The world has capitalized on our fads. When something becomes "in style," the advertisers find many ways to market it. These companies will make us believe that we have to conform to be accepted. We are willing to change our beliefs and stances and do what is popular in this world.

The story of Joseph is so refreshing in a society that wants to tell us that we have to keep up with the Joneses. We have been convinced that if we do not meet the world's standards, we are a lesser cog in the wheel of society. We are told that we must look a certain way, drive a certain car, and live a particular lifestyle to be seen as a success in the eyes of others. Wouldn't it be nice to live in a place where you are viewed by your character and not your looks? There is a way!

To truly win in life, we need to have a solid foundation upon which to build an excellent life. Joseph knew what his foundation was built upon and where. Joseph knew that he was being directed by God and that his circumstances were being led by God. He trusted God enough to know that He was still the same wonderful God whether Joseph was in the pit or ruling a government. You are the same, in God's eyes, no matter your circumstance. You are a beautiful creation of God, and you are the same masterpiece no matter what your life circumstance.

You have heard stories of someone buying a painting at a garage sale and later finding the five-dollar painting to be worth thousands. The painting never changed from what it was; the only thing that changed was its value. You will find that God has made you very valuable, and you just need to let Him place you where He will, and, just like Joseph, you will be valuable to whomever and wherever He places you.

Paul: "Counted All as Joy"

Romans 4:8 says, "Blessed is the man whose sin the Lord will never count against him."

Another figure in the Bible was the apostle Paul. Paul was a man who "counted it as pure joy" no matter what circumstance he was in. In 2 Corinthians 11, we read about Paul's resume of inflictions.

What anyone else dares to boast about—I am speaking as a fool—I also dare to boast about. Are they Hebrews? So am I. Are they Israelites? So am I. Are they Abraham's descendants? So am I. Are they servants of Christ? (I am out of my mind to talk like this.) I am more. I have worked much harder, been in prison more frequently, been flogged more severely, and been exposed to death again and again. Five times I received from the Jews the forty lashes minus one. Three times I was beaten with rods, once I was stoned, three times I was shipwrecked, I spent a night and a day in the open sea, I have been constantly on the move. I have been in danger from rivers, in danger from bandits, in danger from my own countrymen, in danger from Gentiles; in danger in the city, in danger in the country, in danger at sea; and in danger from false brothers. I have labored and toiled and have often gone without sleep; I have known hunger and thirst and have often gone without food; I have been cold and naked. Besides everything else, I face daily the pressure of my concern for all the churches. Who is weak, and I do not feel weak? Who is led into sin, and I do not inwardly burn?

Did you notice that Paul states that "I do not feel weak" and "I do not inwardly burn"? Paul is saying here that no matter what life has thrown him, this world cannot defeat him and that he will not hold a grudge against it. I mean beatings, shipwrecks, jail, labor, and many other things, and Paul is still winning in the game of life.

What a man he must have been. This same Paul had a different heart before he laid his life in the hands of Jesus. Paul was a man who set out on the very road he met Jesus on to persecute and kill those who followed Christ. He was a respected man by his constituents. He was a powerful man for their cause. He was an angry man toward those who followed Christ. He was lacking in character until he met the true Christ and chose to become all he could be. You too can become a changed person who sees life in a different view than the world sees life.

You can rest assured that life is not going to slow down, back off, or allow you a free pass. Life is going to come at you hard. It is going to attack, slam, and try to alter everything about your life. The question then comes down to why, how, and what are we to do about it?

As we explore the win factor over the next few chapters, I want to bring you to a common point. Life was never promised to be easy. No matter your economic or sociological background, life has its own twists and turns. We can allow those twists and turns to either lead our life in a direction of fulfillment or lead our life to a very destructive end.

The Edge

John 19:11 says, "You would have no power over me if it were not given to you from above."

To win in this life, we have to define the word "win." Winning in life cannot be measured by any of the world's standards. The measuring stick must be defined by our attitudes, attempts, perseverance, and cause. In the next chapter, we will begin to look at the "why" of winning and start to define this picture. This will be the edge for winning in this life.

None of us want to lose in this game of life. All of us want to leave a legacy to encourage others and be remembered well. This does not happen by itself. No, this takes intentional living, striving to live the best life we can live. We do not live this life for us; we live this life for Him. Jesus. We must have a goal and direction in life, and most people simply go through life-changing directions with every new philosophy.

A life that truly wins is a life that pursues excellence directly. A life that truly wins does not falter because of location, circumstance, or challenges.

My sister was diagnosed with lymphomas many years ago. The doctors gave her six months to live. My sister is a wonderful Christian woman whom I respect very much. At the time of her diagnosis, she had three wonderful little children.

My sister made a decision, which has impacted my life tremendously: to win over this life and the standards this world sets for us. With God's guidance, she is still with us to this day and has raised those three wonderful children. She lost her youngest to a cyst on the brain when my niece was only seventeen. The courage, love, and perseverance my sister has shown has made her an all-time hero in my life. She understands how life can be cruel, but she has the edge that continues to raise her above what this world will throw at her. When I get the opportunity to get together with her, I always leave her presence feeling better than when I arrived. She chose to win, and that attitude is contagious.

Let me leave you in this chapter with a few simple questions.

- Are you ready to live life to the fullest?

- Will you be willing to accept a better rewards system?

- Can you accept that the world has been telling you a lie?

If so, please continue this journey with me. If not, please stop, pray, and ask God to open your eyes to the possibilities He may have for you and then be willing to listen to Him as He leads.

CHAPTER 2

Why Win?

—ᴍ—

For the Son of Man came to seek and to save what
was lost.

Luke 19:10

I used to coach junior high sports at a private school in
Houston, Texas. We always won more games than we
lost, so I was asked quite often, "How do you teach the kids
to win?" The truth of the matter is I never taught the kids to
win. I simply would ask the kids to have fun, work hard, and
give all they had at the moment. Whether that moment was
practice or game time, I asked them to work hard, have fun,
and to give all they had. I told them to never worry about the
scoreboard, for if they would work hard, have fun, and give
all they had, then the scoreboard would take care of itself. I
explained to them that the score had nothing to do with the
way they performed. Performance was only related to what
they gave and who they gave it for.

I always quoted to my teams 1 Peter 4:11: "If anyone
speaks, he should do it as one speaking the very words of

God. If anyone serves, he should do it with the strength God provides, so that in all things God may be praised through Jesus Christ. To him be the glory and the power for ever and ever. Amen."

Those young boys learned a life lesson of how to win without winning being the focal point. The reason for winning was never about the score or the outcome of the game. Winning became about the principle of living—to live life all out, to lay it all on the line at the moment for the right reasons. These kids are now young men, and even though there are many miles that separate us now, they still contact me and let me know how well they are doing.

These young men have learned a secret about winning. They were taught that winning had everything to do with the why, how, and what we played the game for. We taught the boys to edify their opponent. They were to edify the fans. They were taught to bring glory to God by the way they played. They also understood that the way they handled themselves on the field also would dictate how they would handle life off the field.

Being Consistent

Malachi 3:6 says, "I the LORD do not change."

We tend to separate areas of our life and how we can react and handle those areas. We may react to our friends with a much different attitude than we would a family member. We may put on a separate face for an employee versus our employer. We may refrain from showing our temper in public but explode behind the doors of our home.

To win in life, we must be consistent in how we live this life in all circumstances. Winning has everything to do with the complete life and how it is lived. The first question we have to answer is, Why are we playing the game? Some would say that the game is played to have a winner and a loser. I say we play the game of life so that everyone has the opportunity to taste the sweet taste of victory at some point. Offering consistency to those around us brings stability to everyone's life. Most of our traits are learned behaviors. A learned behavior is a particular way we act, respond, or handle life. Do we communicate well? If not, then it is probably a product of how we observed others communicating throughout our lives. Do we handle conflict well? If not, then we probably didn't have good role models in those areas.

We need to train our behaviors to be steady and constant around others. When we do these things, those around us feel more at ease and are willing to enter into an authentic relationship with us. Most of us only create pseudo relationships with those around us. A pseudo relationship is a relationship where we learn the surface things about people, we speak only of things that will not engage us too deeply, and we hope it will not take up a lot of our time. A pseudo relationship has all of the evidence of a relationship on the surface, but there is no depth. In a pseudo relationship, people withhold themselves from entering in too deeply. We restrain from an authentic relationship.

This holding back may be due to past hurts or failures. The refraining may be due to complex emotions or fears. Whatever the reason may be for pseudo relationships, a pseudo relationship will never be the fulfilling that a heart needs for authentic relationship.

We were made for relationships, and to allow people to enter into a real relationship with us, we need to offer them the safety of being consistent in our attitudes and behaviors. We need to train ourselves to be willing to accept people with the baggage that they may bring into the relationship. We have to be able to accept the baggage that we bring into relationships. We have to be honest with each person and not just do or say what they may want us to do or say. We have to be honest with ourselves. We have to "win" them with our consistency, and we have to "win" ourselves by allowing ourselves to be consistent in life.

A little trick I like to use is "self time out." I have to make myself step back and evaluate a circumstance before I engage. I take a deep breath and ask God, "How can I bring glory to You in this?"

Life can be such an emotional rollercoaster when we allow our emotions to dictate how we handle life. So we must learn how to win over our emotions and allow God to speak right to our hearts. We must be willing to submit to what the Spirit is whispering to us. We must win!

How to "Win"

1 Corinthians 9:19 says, "Though I am free and belong to no man, I make myself a slave to everyone, to win as many as possible."

To understand what we are winning, we have to understand how to win. In most arenas, we win by defeating our opponent, but in life, we should not look at others as the enemy. We should look at others as teammates that we must bring along to a common theme and understanding. Then we will start to see others in a different light. We start to see that cold boss as a person who simply needs love and understanding. Maybe he feels he has never received the respect of his title or the understanding of his vision for the department. When we see our boss as a teammate, then we start to relate and communicate with him in a whole new way.

When we see that relative or neighbor as a help to the cause of life, then we start to relate to them differently. The first move we must make is to be proactive in connecting with people where they are. We must see them for what they can be and put away the notion of who they are. We must see the possibility of what we can win them to be. If the person is not someone who trusts in Christ, then we have to realize that they cannot see the world as we do. The Bible tells us,

"For the message of the cross is foolishness to those who are perishing, but to us who are being saved it is the power of God" (1 Corinthians 1:18). Therefore, we should never be surprised when a nonbeliever cannot see the positive and wonderful things in life when life is not going well.

Often when I counsel couples, I run into the challenge of a believer married to a non-believer. It becomes much clearer to the believing spouse when they understand that the non-believer cannot understand love the way that the believer does. The non-believing spouse has never experienced true love as Christ can impart upon us through grace. The believer starts to see how the understanding of love, as the gospel explains it, is a foreign concept to the non-believing spouse.

The "why" of winning has changed. We are no longer just trying to win the moment for us in life. No, we are trying to win a person to the light. We are trying to show our faith in a way that there is an opportunity for the hand of God to reach down and save someone from the pit of hell. Now, let me stop here for a moment and explain my definition of evangelism. I believe that we evangelize when our lives exhibit the presence of God in all we do. I do not subscribe to attacking a person's life with criticism or guilt.

I believe that if we "love God and love man," then those who are lost will see the reality of the Lord in us without us ever preaching a single word. I have seen over and over someone come to Christ because he sees something special in the way a person has handled the mundane things in life with an unspeakable joy. So I believe that the "why" question is one of salvation for the lost.

I believe the answer to the "how" question is to live life in a way that others cannot refute that the holy living God dwells in you. Live a life where God directs your attitudes. Be willing to share the gospel when the occasion presents itself. Be willing to preach without speaking because the Light of the world is shining through you.

Winning the Believer

Galatians 3:22 says, "But the Scripture declares that the whole world is a prisoner of sin, so that what was promised, being given through faith in Jesus Christ, might be given to those who believe."

You may ask here, "What about the believer—what is there to win for him?"

Winning for the believer is about living life out loud. Just because we have our eternity secured does not give us assurance that life will now be problem-free. We are assured that life will bring us hard times. The question comes to, What will not only get us through hard times, but also give us complete joy in those hard times?

Cami and I have gone through some hard times with our oldest child, Tyler. One month before Tyler turned two, he was diagnosed with a severe staph infection. The doctors conducted two emergency surgeries within a twenty-four hour period. The prognosis was not good. We were told that it was probably in his blood and that he had a high possibility of death. This was quite startling to us. We were young parents and had not had a lot of experience in this arena. I was not about winning at the moment! While my son was in the I.C.U., I went into the hallway and screamed at God.

Yes, I literally screamed at the top of my lungs to the Creator of the universe. I told Him everything I was displeased with. We had just been installed as new pastors in a small church. We were far from our families and support. We did not know anyone really well at this point in the community. We didn't even have a doctor to call our own. In the middle of my rampage with God, I heard a small, still voice. I looked around and saw only a nurse. I did ask if she had said anything. I guess she had not, for she looked as if she was a little afraid of me after my rampage, and she simply said, "No."

I sat on the hallway floor and heard the voice again. I listened, and I knew it was God. He took me down a road and reminded me of several passages of Scripture about how He takes care of everything. Then He reminded me of the story of Abraham and Isaac. You know, the one about how God had asked him to sacrifice his only son. He also reminded me that my son did not belong to me but to Him. I stood up, wiped myself off, marched into my son's room, and gave him back to God right there.

I still did not know about winning then, but within just a few moments, my world was rocked. You see, this couple walked right into my son's I.C.U. room and wanted to know how my son was. They had heard him crying earlier and wanted to know how they could help. I told them his story, and they asked how I was doing. Well, being a pastor and all, I knew the right things to say, so I told them, "He is in God's hands, and no matter what, he will be okay." I never knew how profound that truth really was until they said, "Oh, you're a Christian." I affirmed them, and they asked me what I did for a living. I explained I was a pastor, and then the Lord went to work.

They let me know that their mother was on the fourth floor and dying and asked if I could please go tell her about Jesus. They told me that a man of such faith is just the man that could tell her about God. I didn't have the heart to tell them how weak my faith had become. I went with them and spoke with the woman. I believe that because I was willing to win God's way, God took over and spoke to that woman's heart. That day, an elderly woman accepted Christ. That night, while lying in my son's room on a very uncomfortable chair, my son opened his eyes and spoke to me. We had this little joke. I would call the game of football by its proper name, football. He would smile and call it baseball. The television had a football game on it.

He looked at me and said, "Daddy, football."

I was so excited. I said back to him, "That's right, son, that is football."

My son called it by the right name.

Then, to my surprise, he looked at me and said, "Baseball."

Then he smiled before he went to sleep. I knew my God was doing something very special.

I believe that I learned a large lesson about winning that day. I learned because I was willing to submit to God with my son's life, and I submitted to God and spoke with the woman. As I thought about the events of the day, I acknowledged to God that He won more battles that day than I could have ever fought in a lifetime on my own. I also was very aware that I could never have won any of those battles on my own. It was only with God's power that anything was accomplished that day and every day of my life since.

My son went home a few days later. He went home a very healthy young boy. I still do not know that I understood the "whys" of winning until a few years later. The same son was diagnosed with Chiari malformation Type I.

Chiari is a compression of the brain, and he had to have brain surgery. The "whys" were becoming much clearer to me by this time. As we went forward with this surgery, we were much calmer, more trusting in God. We had a confidence that no matter what happened we have a sovereign God Who has everything under control. We even started to look for what God wanted to do in this very severe moment. After six hours of surgery the news came that the compression was worse than thought, but that he did very well and we could go see him in recovery in just a little while.

I cannot tell you the relief we had, but there was something else there. We had several friends and relatives who came to the hospital to be with us. Because of the growth of the "why" of winning, there was such a wonderful, joyful, sweet spirit that was in that crowd. You see, when you understand that God is up to something in every situation, and that He is in control, and that you cannot lose no matter the circumstance, then we start to affect everyone and every-thing around us. Believers start to grow when we allow them to see the unrestrained Christ in our lives.

I want you to take a moment and reflect upon the fact that God is in total control of your life. Now ask yourself the following questions:

- Am I allowing God to have total control over every situation in my life?

- Do I handle my trials myself first, or do I go to God and trust Him with my trials first?

- Am I willing to give up control of my life to God?

You may wonder how we get to this point. Well, let us look at that in this next chapter on how to win.

CHAPTER 3

How Do I Win Inwardly?

—ɷ—

Do not conform to the pattern of this world, but be
transformed by the renewing of your mind. Then you
will be able to test and approve what God's will is—
his good, pleasing and perfect will.

Romans 12:2

There are two areas of how to win. First, there is the
inward win, and second, there is the outward win. In
this chapter, we will discuss the inward win. You see, you
cannot learn to win the outside world until the inside has
experienced the victory.

Can a Person Change?

Romans 12:2 says, "Do not conform any longer to the
pattern of this world, but be transformed by the renewing of
your mind. Then you will be able to test and approve what
God's will is—his good, pleasing and perfect will."

There was a young girl back in Houston who had strug-
gled with a very rough lifestyle. She was twelve years of age
and was already involved in things I could not imagine. She
did not understand that what she was doing was completely

wrong and the value she placed upon herself was very low. A leader in our church brought her to me and asked if it would be okay for her to attend the youth group that night. When we came to the invitation at the end of the meeting, the young child came forward and asked me to pray with her. I explained to her what grace was, and she asked Christ for that grace.

When we were finished praying, she spoke of how things looked different to her. She stated how she felt free and knew that the lifestyle she had was all wrong. She said that for the first time she felt the strength to quit the life she had and for the first time she knew what she wanted.

Now I have to be honest here, I have seen a lot of conversions, and I did not get too excited. It seems that people can feel pretty brave at the moment, but application is a little harder to come by. That little girl was about to show me true victory. She left that night and immediately quit the lifestyle she had known. She stood in her public school classroom and gave a report on what God had done in her life. She started bringing other troubled kids to church and leading them to Christ. She started going on mission trips and youth camps, and spreading the gospel in her community. Eventually, her entire family came to Christ and became a very active part of our church.

See, this little girl made an inward change. She chose Christ and then was willing to act upon the prompting of the Holy Spirit. I think we forget the leading that God provides for us to win in this life. He gave us the Holy Spirit if we will just listen. You know that still, small voice that the world will call a conscience? Listen to God. He has provided a built-in coach to lead us to victory over the world. Everyone who accepts Christ is given the Holy Spirit as a Comforter.

Can people change? Yes! People can be changed by the wonderful work of Christ. If we tried to do the changing on our own, we would most likely fail. But, through the miraculous power of Jesus Christ, we can overcome any lifestyle, attitude, and addiction.

Philippians 4:13 tells us, "I can do everything through him who gives me strength." This means that with the power of the Holy Spirit, there is nothing I cannot accomplish. The world can throw as much dirt at me as it wants, but the world cannot defeat what Christ is doing in me.

I am not sure we want to let go of the lies of the world. It may seem that we want to hang on to the things of this world. We are told to tithe, but we want to hold on to what God is asking for. We want to volunteer, but we don't want it to take our time. We want to encourage, but we are afraid of how someone will respond. We want to accept and follow Christ, but we are afraid of what it will take on our part. The Holy Spirit will tug on you and try to prompt you to believe, react, and follow all of the Lord's ways.

The biggest problem we seem to have is that we ignore this prompting and make decisions based upon the standards of the world. The world has only promised us destruction, but God has given us the promise of victory over this world. The first step in achieving the how of winning is to accept Christ as your Savior and get on the winning team.

I want to stop for a moment. Some people make this step very complicated, but it is not. Romans 10:9 tells us, "If you confess with your mouth, 'Jesus is Lord,' and believe in your heart that God raised him from the dead, you will be saved." The key here is confession and believing. If you have not taken this step, and if you are ready, put this book down and simply do those two things. If you have done this, I want to congratulate you and commend you on the wisest decision you have ever made. If you made that decision today, I would love to hear from you.

Being Empowered

Acts 1:8 says, "But you will receive power when the Holy Spirit comes on you."

Now that you have won the first victory, let us talk about continuing to win inwardly. You have to realize that as a believer, you have tapped into a power that the world cannot harness. To be empowered, you must be willing to act upon what the Lord is telling you. If you have been gifted in an area and you are not using that gift, my question to you is, Why not? The "how" of winning comes when you are willing to move forward at the request of the Most High. You grow to be able to handle the things that life throws at you when you have experienced more and more life experiences.

You can win inwardly when you stop seeing yourself as the world dictates—fame, power, money, popularity, etc.— and you start seeing yourself for what you are becoming in Christ. You cannot be effective for the long term outwardly until you allow God to have the victory over you inwardly. Every one of us fights our own inward battles. You know, those things that you keep locked away from everyone else. You know, those thoughts that only you and God know about. When we let God be Master over all of those areas of our lives, then we start to experience a confidence and understanding about ourselves that we have never experienced before. When we finally start to allow God to take over our lives, we start to learn how to "win" outwardly.

Every one of us has a corner in our lives that we keep locked away. We allow God to have control over other areas, but not that one. You say, "I can handle this one." The truth is that you cannot handle it. You may lie to yourself for a while, but eventually, it becomes too big of a burden for you to carry. You have to start by telling God what the issue is. Trust Him. Tell Him. You will feel much better after you tell Him. Then go the next step. Give it to Him. Stop carrying the burden, and just lay it at His feet and walk away. God is making you into a winner. Let Him.

Remember what the Bible says in Romans 8:37: "No, in all these things we are more than conquerors through him who loved us." You have been empowered with a power that the world cannot defeat. You have been set apart for a perfect work.

Before we move to our next chapter about outwardly winning, take a moment to truly reflect on how you see yourself.

- Do you gauge yourself by the standards of the world or by the understanding of what God is making you into?

- Can you accept that you have been empowered by the Holy Spirit to carry out the service that God has called you to?

Take a moment and really think about this question. How we actually gauge our lives is very important. Pray that you may see yourself as God sees you.

CHAPTER 4

The How of Outwardly Winning

—ɷ—

For physical training is of some value, but godliness
has value for all things, holding promise for both the
present life and the life to come.

1 Timothy 4:8

As an athlete prepares before a big game, so must we
prepare to win the game of life. I can remember sitting
in the locker room before a high school soccer game. The
coach would have us close our eyes. He would explain to
us that the training had already taken place and that now we
must prepare our minds for the task ahead of us. We would
sit there with our eyes closed and just go through the motions
of a complete game as we prepared to take on our opponent.
When we opened our eyes, we had a pretty good visual of
what the game should look like.

To bring others to the knowledge that they, too, can
defeat the world by being in Christ, we must know how to
bring them to this knowledge. We must have a game plan to
enter into this arena.

Fellowship

1 John 1:7 says, "But if we walk in the light, as he is in the light, we have fellowship with one another, and the blood of Jesus, his Son, purifies us from all sin."

I believe there are three things a believer needs to be involved in to prepare himself for outwardly winning. The first is being a part of a healthy, encouraging fellowship of believers. There is something about being around people who believe and support you in Christ. When you have a support system of people who encourage and build you up, then you will have more confidence to face a pretty scary world. Being a part of such a fellowship is a boost to your very soul. To have the confidence that there will be a group of people that will be consistent with their time, wisdom, caring, support, and love is a very secure and nurturing thing. The greatest part of this is that you can be who God truly made you to be. You can practice being that person, so you can put away your facades that you put on for the world.

Remember the story of my son and the brain surgery? One of the things that made it so different from the first surgery was the number of people who were at the hospital to support us. The relationships of believers helped us with our confidence in facing a very tough experience. Even as pastor, I did not have to put on a pastoral face at the hospital. I was simply me, a father who cared for his son's health and welfare.

In Acts 2, it tells us "that they met in their homes daily." What true fellowship that must have been—eating meals together, praying for one another, learning from one another, and all of this daily. That is a true support group, and what an encouragement to the soul it must have been. If you do not have a church home or find too many excuses to not be a part of a church, I would encourage you to search the Word and seek a good church fellowship to practice your gifts in.

Get involved in a local fellowship. Allow God to use the wonderful way He has made you to add to the family of that fellowship. Do not forsake the church that God has created. Encourage the body of Christ by your presence and involvement.

Winning Through Growing

2 Corinthians 10:15 says, "Neither do we go beyond our limits by boasting of work done by others. Our hope is that, as your faith continues to grow, our area of activity among you will greatly expand."

The second suggestion I would have is to go deeper. To truly win outwardly, we must learn the Word and know how to apply it. Without a Bible study, small group, Sunday school, or some type of more in-depth study, we cannot be properly prepared to live out the victory. Even with all the enthusiasm we can muster, we cannot be effective for the long term without knowledge. Most people who are new to Christ have an amazing excitement about them. They are so much fun to be around as they share what God has done in their lives. The downside to this is that it seems to fizzle out pretty quickly without proper guidance and leading of a more mature Christian in their lives. Without the guidance of Scripture, instruction, and other more mature believers, it becomes ever more difficult to grow. To truly prepare to win outwardly, we must prepare inwardly.

I want to encourage you to allow yourself to be taught. Find a way to allow yourself to study the Word and listen to the wisdom of a more mature believer. Grow through relationships with other believers, and look for others to bounce areas of non-understanding off of.

Paul, when the scales were removed from his eyes, sat under the teaching of the apostles. In Acts 2, we read that the believers sat under the teaching of the apostles. We need to be taught the Word, and we need to have a firm understanding of the Word.

I cannot tell you how many times when a crisis has arisen that God has reminded me of a Scripture, a story, or the words of another believer. These reminders come from the study and fellowship that comes from going deeper. We grow deeper through fellowship, study, prayer, and commitment to these areas.

Getting Into the Game

1 Peter 4:13 says, "But rejoice that you participate in the sufferings of Christ, so that you may be overjoyed when his glory is revealed."

The third aspect of winning outwardly is to discover your spiritual gifts and put them to use. Now, some of you reading this are sure about your passions and gifts, and some of you are not. There are wonderful tools to help you discover your gifts. I encourage you to truly seek out your gifts, but also remember knowledge is not enough. One of the best ways to win outwardly is for others to see you working in your gifts. When people work in their gifts, they work in an area of passion. They enjoy what they are doing, and that is contagious.

People are exposed to your joys and are being blessed by your gifts. When this happens, it opens a person to ponder the whys of what you are doing. They seem to want to talk or hang around. Working in your gifts gives others the opportunity to receive from you what God has already done inside of you.

You see, most people really want relationships, and when you share in your gifts, it opens doors that would have never been open for people to interact in a relationship with you. You do not have to be on the stage or be the leader of a group. You do not have to stand on a soap box and scream out the gospel. You simply have to be willing to put your faith into action.

When I was in a church in Akron, Ohio, there was a little old lady who watered the plants every Sunday. She brought two milk jugs full of water every Sunday and placed them under her pew. After the service, she would march around the church singing children's songs and would water the plants. I noticed that after some time, the kids started following her. They would follow her, singing those songs and helping her water the plants. These kids were enjoying her gifts and at the same time learning about Christ. I cannot tell you how many adults were blessed by the sight of this as well.

Being encouraged by fellowship, growing through learning, and using your gifts will help you win outwardly in ways you could never imagine. God has wonderful plans for us, and we cannot always see the plan until He has unfolded it.

In the next chapter, we will talk about what we are to win. Before we move on, let me ask you a few questions if I may. Take a moment, read the questions, and then pray for God's guidance and be honest with Him and yourself.

- Have I allowed God to win me inwardly?

- Have I trusted Him with my whole life?

- Am I allowing God to use me to win my family members?

- Do I trust in Him to win those around me in my life?

- What must I do in my life to allow God to lead me to win others to Him?

Now that we have a better picture of how to win outwardly, I want us to take a look at those we are to win.

CHAPTER 5

Who Are We to Win?

—ℳ—

For whoever wants to save their life will lose it, but
whoever loses their life for me will find it.

Matthew 16:25

Who are we to win? That is a question we all must
face. In the last chapter we spoke about why we win
family, friends, and others. I want to talk about who we are
to win in this chapter.

The Lost

Luke 19:10 says, "For the Son of Man came to seek and
to save what was lost."

The lost are those who have not made Jesus the Lord and
Savior of their life. It sounds broad, but you can decipher
who these people may be. If you have a good relationship
with these people, you can ask them straight out if they have
accepted Christ as their Savior. This, however, can be a very
uncomfortable experience for most people. I would suggest
you get to know the person well enough to watch their life
up close.

Notice the things that are important to them. Notice the things they pursue in life. Notice what has become number one in their life. See if they have a church life, prayer life, devotional life. Watch the kinds of places where they like to go and what they like to do. After just a short time, you will see a pattern of pursuing God or pursuing of the world. It becomes very clear what priorities people have when you start to be around them more.

Now, I am not saying to judge their lives and condemn them to hell. No, I am saying to examine their life in a way that you can be prepared to present the gospel and encourage them to consider joining the team. Remember, our goal is to bring as many people to the team as possible. Each person will bring something to the team that will build up the body of Christ. So get to know the person, and eventually, the Holy Spirit will open opportunities for dialogue. When the Holy Spirit presents the opportunity, you need to be prepared. This again is why study is so important. Be prepared to give an answer when the opportunity arises.

Know your story. Your story is what people really want to hear. They want to know what God has done in your life and why you believe. People will want to know that this is not just a thought but that it actually happened to you. Be prepared to give your story of what God has done in your own life.

Pray for the person who is lost. When we pray for people specifically, we seem to grow in affection for the person being prayed for. Pray for them every day. Pray for God to open opportunities to show them the way to Christ. Pray that they will accept the message of the cross. Pray that you will be willing to walk through the door that God opens.

The odds are that if a person who is lost engages in a relationship with you, then that person eventually will feel comfortable enough to discuss spiritual matters with you. We underestimate the lost way too much. We need to remember that they are lost! When you are lost, you want to know a way to your destination. Lost people want to know what they're lost to and how to find where they are going. Some people will not even know they are lost until they are exposed to someone who is found.

Remember the young girl in the last chapter? We never preached to her and told her that she was doomed to hell. No, we simply loved her and enjoyed her; we got to know her and her lifestyle. She started to see there was a better way, and she opened the door to go the better way. She is now winning in the game of life. Is she perfect? No, she is not, but she is striving toward the prize and understands that she is never alone and that God is in control.

Get to know those who are lost around you, reach out to them, and exhibit Christ and the way He wants us to pursue life.

Winning Strangers

Job 29:16 says, "I was a father to the needy; I took up the case of the stranger."

We should win those we do not know. This may sound a bit odd, but as we discussed in the last chapter, people are watching our lives. As a pastor in a small town, I cannot sneeze without a person yelling, "God bless you, pastor." I am aware 24/7 of my actions, attitudes, and behaviors. It is part of the position in life I serve, and most people think that is fine for the pastor, but we all must acknowledge that others are watching us as well. Christ sees all of us as in the priesthood.

Well, if you are a believer, you have made that choice. Peter tells us in 1 Peter 2:9, "But you are a chosen people, a royal priesthood, a holy nation, a people belonging to God, that you may declare the praises of him who called you out of darkness into his wonderful light." Every one of us who has decided to follow Jesus has become a "royal priesthood."

We have been set apart to do His will, for it is He Who has brought us out of the destructive life we were living. We must live a life that reflects what He has done. Others are watching you. I do not care if you think you are popular or not; there is someone watching you.

Think about that for a moment—who may be watching you? Do you have a small child who is watching you? Do you have a coworker watching you? Do you have a store clerk whom you see at the local Stop-N-Shop on a regular basis? There is someone who thinks you are important and has a preconceived notion about you that is probably much different than how you see yourself.

I remember watching the varsity football players at the local high school when I was in middle school. I tried to imitate their swagger and the way they dressed and talked. I wanted to be like them, and they never knew who I was. I watched them on the field at Friday night games. I saw them in the store and watched what they were buying. I saw them in the neighborhood and how they interacted with one another. Someone is watching you like that. You may never know it, but someone may want to be you in some aspect.

That person may be lost, and you may say or do the one thing that turns them toward or away from Christ. You may say at this point, "This is way too much pressure to live by." Maybe this is too much pressure, but if we live the life as to "win the prize," we do not even realize we are doing these things. If our life truly is pursuing the prize of heaven and reflecting what the Lord has done, then we start to naturally live this life out loud.

I would encourage you to reflect on how you affect others with whom you may come into contact on a daily basis and ask yourself, "How am I doing?" This is a tough place to go because you will most likely not like everything you see about yourself. Ask the Lord to expose the things that do not need to be in your life and to replace those things with the things that should be in your life.

As we live our life upon this earth, we must allow Christ to win the battle over our lives by accepting Him, to win the battle over other lives by allowing Him to work through us, and ultimately to win the prize, which is heaven and the rewards He has stored up for us there.

Winning the Believer

John 13:15 says, "I have set you an example that you should do as I have done for you."

Now, the concept of winning someone who is already a believer sounds a little out of the ordinary. I want you to understand that I am not directing you to convert them to Christianity. We are assuming that they are believers already at this time. I am encouraging you to win them to pursue a deeper relationship with Christ and others. The church is filled with pew warmers. You know, those people who come to church on Sunday and never lift a finger for the Lord at any other time.

I want to encourage you to motivate, encourage, direct, lead, assist, and whatever else it may take to get that person to engage in the game. I can remember a little guy I coached in middle school soccer. He would wear his watch to the games and would set it to the game time. He would repeatedly tell me, from the bench, how much time was left in the game. He would remind me of the score. He would even tell me when someone was looking fatigued or injured.

He knew by continually doing this that I was aware that he was present and willing to go in. Now, his skills were not what the other kids' were, but his heart was willing. I made sure I got him into the game at some time, and when I did, the fans went crazy. They loved it when he came into the game. The team played better to take up the slack of his position. The enthusiasm of the whole game would change.

We can be this same type of blessing that this young boy was to the team to those in our lives when we just encourage them to get involved. Each believer has the potential to do something absolutely incredible for Christ. Our lives must encourage them to use the gifts, passions, and abilities the Lord has given them.

Ask yourself:

• Do I exhibit a life to lead others to Christ?

• Am I aware of the lost in my life?

• Am I conscious that others are watching my example?

Our next chapter will deal with the idea of building for the kingdom of Christ. Again, I want to encourage you to contact me if anything in this book has touched you. I want to hear your story, and I want to encourage and be encouraged by you. Let us look at "building."

CHAPTER 6

What Are We to Win?

—∿—

Stand firm, and you will win life.

Luke 21:19

Every game that is played, every deal that is won, every fight that is fought has a goal: to win! We are a society that is taught to win. To be taught to win is not a bad thought, but at what cost? is the true question. We sometimes lose sight of the prize of winning. We seem to be willing to compromise our values, ethics, morals, and time simply to win. By winning this way, we forget what it is we are truly trying to win.

Christ said, "I came to serve, not be served." When we start to see others as the object of our service, then we start to see them through the eyes of the almighty Creator of the universe. Every business, sports team, nonprofit agency, government agency, and individual has a goal to pursue. Our goal of living a life that is excellent has many different goals, and each goal is from a different view than the world has.

The Goal of Self

Ephesians 4:22 says, "You were taught, with regard to your former way of life, to put off your old self, which is being corrupted by its deceitful desires."

The first goal we will discuss is the goal of self. The goal of self is "pressing on toward the prize," as Paul states. We have to realize that this world is not our goal. This world only has temporal prizes to offer us. Yes, it is true, we can leave a legacy to those left behind. We can leave a legacy of what the world can give us, things such as fame, possessions, power, money, lust, physical pleasure, etc. What we physically leave behind is a temporary fix. We will pass on from this world, and then what?

If a businessperson only planned his business to be successful for a day, then he would quickly go out of business. If a team planned for only one game and not a season, there would be no quest for a championship. I think you get the point. In this life, we must plan for the future. Some of us do that by a 401k or a portfolio. Some of us invest in real estate or some other type of investment. We watch it grow with the expectation of it maturing and us one day retiring. Our lives do have a goal to win beyond what we can see upon this earth. Our prize is the rewards God has stored up for us in heaven.

God is watching our lives upon this earth, and He is going to reward us in heaven for what we did with the knowledge of Him and the gifts He gave us while upon this earth. We need to pursue life on this earth with heaven as the goal. When we live life with the cross of glory in the backdrop, we see challenges, people, labor, illness, death, joy, triumph, and loss in a completely different way.

We cannot let life build our egos up too much or tear us down too low. We must see that God has a plan in everything that exists in our life, and we must know that "we are more than conquerors" when we allow Him to be sovereign in our lives. We must remain humble, yet triumphant in this life. When we can get to that place where to win in life is to please God and not man or ourselves, then we find ourselves in a place of peace.

There was a lady back in Houston who went to the doctor for some tests. She had been ill off and on and could not understand why. After the tests were returned, the doctor notified her that she had cancer and six months to live and that treatment may even shorten that time.

Looking right at the doctor, she exclaimed, "Praise the Lord!"

The doctor was shocked and asked, "Why are you so happy? I have never had anyone respond like this."

She replied, "I know when I get to see my Jesus."

What peace we can have when we know what we are to win and know that can override anything in our earthly lives.

The Goal for Others

Mark 4:20 says, "Others, like seed sown on good soil, hear the word, accept it, and produce a crop—thirty, sixty or even a hundred times what was sown."

The second area I want to talk about is the goal for others. We have so many different dynamics of people that come in and out of our lives. Those people we have family relationships with and those who are like family. Those people we have professional relationships with and those who are neighbors and simply passing through our lives. There are those we never meet face to face but are watching from afar.

In 2001, there was a national news case where a lady was caught on tape spanking her child violently. This lady was labeled immediately as a terrible mother. No one in my circles knew this lady, but everyone had an opinion. Now, I do not know what type of person this lady was, and her act of violence was not to be tolerated, but at the same time, millions of people were influenced by her behavior.

I want you to know that there are people you will never meet who will stick with you for the rest of your life. You will make an impression upon somebody watching from afar. I know in the summer of 2000, I was leading a high school Bible study at a local Starbucks. There was a kid who was not with our group who was seated a few tables away and was listening to our discussion. I felt the Holy Spirit prompting me to go talk to this young man after our study. I was uncomfortable with this thought. The young man caught my eye a couple of times, and I turned away quickly. Once the study was complete, I left rather quickly to avoid the young man. I have felt tremendous guilt ever since that day, and I can only pray that his "from afar" observations planted a seed and that my aloofness did not turn him away.

I want to encourage you to win those by our life who we don't even know. I cannot tell you how many people who will never attend the local Sunday sermon whom you will have an opportunity to lead to Christ. There are people who simply observe your life without ever interacting. Watch for those people, and listen to the prompting of the Holy Spirit. Act upon those leadings. Do not be like me and walk away quickly.

The next group that we should look to win, and not in any order, is those we do know. The family unit is unlike any other relationship out there. We seem to be able to hurt, love, encourage, tear down, and sometimes even despise those in our own families. Yet, with all of that, we still can remain in love with those members of our family. I have found that the hardest thing for a family to do is relay God's love in their own homes. Whatever the reason, we hold back and refrain and sometimes even hope the church will do this job for us.

We need to understand that the responsibility to bring our family to Christ is laid upon us. We must make a decision that "as for me and my house, we will serve the Lord." Once we make this decision, we must see our family as the most important target of our God affection. We must teach, rebuke, love, encourage, and excite them about following Christ.

I work with the fire department and police department as a chaplain in our small town. I see families that are totally out of control on a regular basis. I have been pastoral counseling for several years and have seen Christian homes just as out of control. In both cases, we see the sins of the parents repeated in the children and in their children as well. We need to stop the cycle by assaulting an all out force of Christian guidance in our homes. No one can make an impact upon a child like a parent.

I have found in my experience that more often than not, no matter how well a program at the church functions, what happens at home overrides anything we do as a church. There is a saying, "Do as I say and not as I do." This has destroyed more homes than drugs, alcohol, etc. A child will almost always do what you do versus what you say. Life lessons are more "caught than taught." Live the Christian life you want your children to follow, and most likely, you will win them to the prize of heaven as well.

This same influence of living the life will affect those you have relationships with outside of the family unit as well. When you model the life in the way you respond at work, then your coworker will see this attitude and either follow or inquire as to why. When you model it at the softball game, in the marketplace, in your yard, at church, on vacation, and any other place where you may get to have relationships, you start setting a precedent to live an excellent life. Your family will pick up on these attitudes toward life.

We have a softball team as part of our church activities, and we had a young lady join our team. This young lady was not part of our church at the time. She was fun to be around, and she could really play softball. We just welcomed her in and played ball with her. She started to notice that we didn't get mad, curse, or scream when things didn't go our way. She watched for almost a whole season to see if we would slip up or if it was a good act. At the end of the season, she came up to me in the dugout and said she wanted to speak. The game had just ended, and the next team wanted in the dugout.

I asked her what was on her mind, and she said that she had learned so much about being a Christian by watching the members of this team, and she wanted to accept Christ and be that way too. As she buried her head in my chest, we prayed together, and she accepted Christ right there in that dugout. She is a part of our church and a part of our lives.

You never know the impact of who you can win and encourage when you live a life that gives every opportunity to those around you to see how Christ is shining through you. We can allow them to see how Christ is changing each of us and how He is helping you to win this game of life.

Take a moment and reflect on the impact you may have on others.

* Do they know you are a Christian at your work by the way you interact with others?

* Would they know you are a Christian in your community?

I want to encourage you to be aware of the lost in your life. The lost come in and out of it every day. Pray that the Lord will open your eyes to the opportunities of the lost in your life.

CHAPTER 7

Build

—⟋⟍—

Teaching them to obey everything I have commanded you.

Matthew 28:20a

1 Peter 2:6 says, "See, I lay a stone in Zion, a chosen and precious cornerstone, and the one who trusts in him will never be put to shame." The cornerstone, I have learned, is the most important piece of a building. The weight of the building rests upon the cornerstone. If the cornerstone is weak, the whole building will have problems. We must acknowledge that we have to build upon the work Christ has done in us through salvation.

The Concept to Build

Luke 14:28 says, "Suppose one of you wants to build a tower. Will he not first sit down and estimate the cost to see if he has enough money to complete it?"

The concept to build is no different than when we look to build a home. The first step is to make the decision to build. Then we move to the planning stage. We look at the needs, resources, cost, place to build upon, and builder to use. We will assume at this point you have chosen Christ as the builder. To build, we must have a place to serve, look at our resources, inventory the needs, and count the physical, emotional, and time restraint cost.

The decision to build is not the decision to accept the gift of salvation. We will assume that grace has already taken place in your life. The decision to build is when you reach a place where you are ready to grow in your faith. It is that moment when you come to a point to want to know more about Christ and your relationship with Him. You have given Him your life, and now it is time to live out that commitment.

This was a hard place for me. I was twelve when I accepted Christ. Deciding to study the Bible, sit in a class, or listen to others was not an easy place for me. It was a long, slow, and sometimes tedious process. It was not until I was much older that I found myself incomplete. I was incomplete in my ability to know what I really believed. I was incomplete in my ability to defend my faith. And I was incomplete in my ability to tell others about my Jesus. I came to a place where I knew I needed to go deeper.

Each of us will come to this point. The problem is, most of us will do nothing about it.

We must make our plans as to how we are going to build. We need to look at what is available in our lives. There are things such as time, Bible studies, friends, pastors, church leaders, books, and other materials that can assist us in our growth. We need to access what we can do to grow. I am a reader and enjoy going deeper through study and reading outside resources. You may prefer to sit under a teacher. You may enjoy a one-on-one study. There are many ways to go deeper, and you must find the way that fits you.

You must build upon the truth. There are a lot of misleading philosophies out there. Make sure that what you are building on is founded upon Jesus Christ. The best way to do this is to test it against the Word. Your cornerstone must be Christ. If what you are studying does not align properly with the Word, I would advise you to run as fast as you can away from it! Build upon the solid rock of Jesus Christ, your Cornerstone.

Preparing to Build

Mark 1:3 says, "A voice of one calling in the desert, 'Prepare the way for the Lord, make straight paths for him.'"

Each of us who has been won by Christ has come to a starting point in our lives. We have been given a new "cornerstone." Where we once carried all of the weight and burden of life on our own shoulders, He, Jesus Christ, has lifted those burdens and has given us a new outlook toward how we face life.

Let me remind you that life is not going to take it easy on you just because you are a Christian. If anything, life will be a little harder on you because you believe in the truth of Christ. This world has Satan running loose upon it. Satan is the "prince of this world," according to John 12:31. We should not be surprised that this world is full of deceit and lies.

To combat this world, we need to be prepared. We cannot get by with luck. My high school soccer coach, Alan Baker, had a wonderful saying about luck. He said, "Luck is simply preparation meeting opportunity." I do not personally believe in luck. I believe in divine intervention, and I believe that we need to be as prepared as we can for every endeavor.

I agree with coach: We need preparation for every opportunity. If we build our cornerstone upon Christ and His Word, then we will be able to get through, or handle most circumstances that come our way. I can tell you many stories of people who have gone through amazing situations and experienced great victory. I also can tell you many episodes where people suffered great defeat due to a lack of understanding of their own faith.

The Bible tells us that we must "continue to work out your salvation with fear and trembling" (Philippians 2:12). We should understand from this that it is an ongoing process. This should also remind us that the road will not always be easy. As we look at this Scripture, it should make us look at our lives and see if we are "working out our salvation."

To work it out, we must first work. To work out our salvation means we must build it up. In today's society, we have become spiritually lazy. We expect the Sunday morning sermon to give us all we need to build our faith. We want to go to church to receive something from the service or to socialize with others. We need to grasp the concept that to build our faith, we need to know what needs to be built and how to go about it. We need to be intentional about building our faith. We must exercise our faith on a regular basis.

The word "work" indicates that we must physically take part in our faith. We should read God's Word; study His ways; physically, emotionally, and spiritually put our faith to work. We should work with other believers in our faith. We can look forward to exercising our faith as we interact with non-believers.

We must also work out our faith with "fear and trembling." This is not a type of fear that brings anxiety. This is a fear of respect and adoration to the Father of creation. We should grow in our salvation with respect toward the Father, Son, and Holy Spirit. We do this by acknowledging that our very breath is only possible because He allows it. We know that any knowledge, wisdom, ability, and passion we have is only because He has set it in our hearts. We must reverently respect and honor Him with our faith.

We must stop going to worship services and Bible studies to receive something. We must attend these services with the mind-set that we are going to give our worship to the King of kings. We are a society that looks to receive. We need to become people who look to give. We must change our thought process and prepare the soil for His service, and then we must break ground.

Breaking Ground

Job 21:33 says, "The soil in the valley is sweet to him; all men follow after him, and a countless throng goes before him."

We need to decide to move forward with our faith and stop being a pew warmer. There is no way to build the faith if we do not exercise our faith. My father had a garage built. I went by about every other day and watched the process of the building of this garage. I noticed that the slowest process was the preparation of the ground. The builder prepared the soil. He measured the area. He marked exactly where he was going to dig. I noticed how meticulous the builder was about getting the ground ready before he began to break the ground for construction.

The farmer prepares the ground before he plants. He may spray for unwanted growth. He may till the ground to prepare the soil. He may apply insecticides. When he has prepared the ground so it has the best opportunity to produce a good crop, the farmer then will start to plant his seed.

We need to make sure that after we accept Christ as our Savior, we are just as meticulous about building the new person God is making us into. Too many people teach that salvation is enough. When Jesus calls us to Him, we have to acknowledge that He has called us to service as well. We have to be willing to say to God, "You have called me to follow you; now lead me to where you want me to go."

Each of us, once we have accepted Christ, should step back and take a good look at our lives. We should look at what is important to us and why it is important. We need to evaluate if those things bring glory to God or to man. We will start to see what needs to be changed and what needs to be redirected to honor God. It was not until many years after

I accepted Christ that I realized how selfish I was. It took a while for me to notice that I was self-focused and not God-focused. We have to look at the very core of who we are, just as a builder looks at the ground to make sure it will hold the weight of the building he will build. The farmer evaluates the soil before he plants his crop.

We have to prepare the soil for what He is going to grow in and through us. We have to allow Christ to start a work in us so he can "break ground" and start to build in us a foundation. We have to allow Him to ready the ground so He can plant the seeds to produce a good crop.

To follow means we actually have to move. I have to admit, I am not good with directions. When I travel with my family, my wife has to navigate. If I had to navigate and drive, I would remain lost. Cami is great with a map, and I trust her fully. To build our faith, we have to realize there are different areas we need to develop. We need to build the foundation. We need to build the gifts and talents and passions we have. We also have to build others. None of the building that needs to take place can take place if we are not willing to grow.

Take a look at where you are. Do you like the produce that you are producing? Have your vines withered? For a moment, allow yourself to be honest and really seek out what God is pointing out to you. Prepare yourself to be used by the Almighty to accomplish what only He can through you. God wants to break ground and begin a good work in you.

In the next chapter, we are going to look at the foundation of building. Before we go there, I want to ask you a couple of questions:

- Are you willing to grow in your relationship with Christ?

- Are you willing to do the work necessary to "work out your salvation"?

- Can you take the time to become what He is calling you to be?

If the answer is yes, I want to encourage you. You are about to go on a ride that will, not can, change your life forever. Now hang on because here we go!

CHAPTER 8

The Foundation

—⟶⟵—

Therefore everyone who hears these words of mine
and puts them into practice is like a wise man who
built his house on the rock.

Matthew 7:24

The foundation is the most crucial element of living a
truly great life in Christ. We must first grasp that God is
in control and can be fully trusted. Many Christians say this,
but very few practice it. To practice this, it means we have
to understand that no matter how great or how horrific the
situation may seem, we are okay because God has already
worked it all out.

We need to get to the place that we are not controlled
by our emotions, but trust in a sovereign Lord totally. Then
and only then can we see life in a light that exposes the
world's weakness and acknowledges the strength of God in
all circumstances. The light of Christ will expose all truths.

Emotions

Titus 2:12 says, "It teaches us to say 'No' to ungodliness and worldly passions, and to live self-controlled, upright and godly lives in this present age."

I want to spend just a moment on emotions. Emotions are a very healthy part of our lives. They allow us to experience such things as joy, peace, sadness, happiness, sorrow, anxiety, fear, and many other wonderful moments in life. But emotions are a part of our makeup; emotions are not our makeup. We were designed to experience different emotions, but we were not designed for those emotions to control our decisions, attitudes, or futures.

Fighter pilots are in a very high-tension job. When a pilot is engaged by enemy fire, there are things called endorphins that begin to kick in. He feels the adrenaline and wants to react. He cannot react to the emotion. No, the fighter pilot has to take a deep breath, assess the situation, and make a sound decision based upon his training.

We are no different. When trials come into our life, we must not react on emotions. We must react after we reflect upon our training. Christians in America have become lazy in our training. We do not take learning about our faith and how to defend and present our faith seriously at all. Now don't get mad if you do not agree with me. Just look around at our society. We do a very good job of evangelizing, but a very poor job of educating people in their faith.

Reacting with emotions is just so much easier, it seems. It requires no forethought. It requires no study. Reacting with emotions doesn't even require us to seek guidance. All it requires is that we react and allow the chips to fall where they may. Once the smoke has settled, then we go to work to find a way to justify our actions.

Justifying our actions usually comes back to how someone made us feel or how they hurt us. To really live a great life in Christ, we must first be willing to build a foundation in ourselves that is based upon the Word of God. To do this, we must be intentional with reading and studying His Word. This can be carried out in many ways.

When we know the Word of God, we can react to situations in life with a calm assurance of the truth. We can measure our reaction against the Word of God. We can make decisions based upon the guidance of Scripture and not on emotions. This will not always be popular with the worldview, but it will always be right. We will please our heavenly Father and gain in strength with our faith. When we stand upon the Word, we also start to experience a growth from the inside out.

Growing

Deuteronomy 32:2 says, "Let my teaching fall like rain and my words descend like dew, like showers on new grass, like abundant rain on tender plants."

There are many ways you can grow. You can get involved in a Bible study, a discussion group, a home group study, a self study, and many other options that may be available. When a new believer comes to me and asks what they should do, I always direct him to get involved in the three aspects of spiritual growth; fellowship, study, and involvement make up these three aspects. Remember, we spoke about them earlier in the book?

Make a commitment to go to worship services, go deeper through the study of the Word, and discover your gifts and start to work in them. The first part was a commitment. Without being committed to growing, you will not grow. Growth does not just happen. Growth is intentional.

I have been ministering and counseling for a long time now, and I still find myself feeling inadequate at times. I may get asked a question and I cannot even think of where to send the person biblically. I may be counseling a person and not have a clue what to say. These are the times that I am encouraged to know that there are parts of my knowledge that I still need to work on.

Even though I know I need to work on them, at the very least, I should know where I need to go. Simply knowing this is not enough. After the person leaves, I set apart some time and I go to work. I look up passages, I search commentaries, and I even go online and search for information. I may call a more seasoned Christian. There is always a part of my lack of knowledge being exposed, and I have to continually work on my understanding of the gospel. Our personal foundation in Christ needs to be built.

Now let's get to it. The foundation can be built through knowledge, as I have just spoken about. I also believe our foundation is built by personal experience. The apostle Paul had his foundation torn apart by a personal experience. He was on the road to Damascus when he had a personal experience with Jesus Christ. The moment literally left him blinded. He immediately had to rely on others for everything. This personal experience that blinded him allowed him to see the true light, which was Jesus Christ. Once he obeyed God and allowed God to make a way for his eyes to see again, he immediately subjected himself to the teaching of those who already believed.

This personal experience laid a foundation of faith in Paul. He was willing to do whatever was needed for others to understand that they needed to experience Jesus as well. Now, your experience may not be one of the physical magnitudes of Paul's, but rest assured, this life will bring us experiences. When we start to learn from these times and realize that God is controlling every happening, we also start to strengthen the foundation of trust in Christ. We start to look at situations as blessings rather than curses.

I have been encouraged by the personal experiences of a young lady. Her name was Haley, and she was my niece. Haley had been diagnosed as a small child with an arachnid cyst in her brain. It could not be cut out, and the only option was to shunt it for as long as they could. This diagnosis meant that she would be very susceptible to infections, eye problems, pain, and many other side effects.

This would have held most people back and brought them to the point of depression. Not our Haley! She was a true go-getter! She took on life in all arenas. She was a straight A student in school, even when she would miss many days. She was on the flag team for her high school. She collected dolls. She would trick other kids into coming to her home so she could conduct Bible studies.

Haley and I, when she was not to leave the house for medical reasons, snuck away for a few hours and went shopping for prom dresses and ate out at her favorite Mexican eatery. She blessed everyone's life who knew her. When Haley was seventeen, there was nothing the doctors could do for her any longer. Everyone around her was sad and depressed. Not Haley. She was always upbeat and encouraging.

She would ask for ice cream, and I would go get it for her. When she could no longer manipulate the spoon, she would not allow us to help her. She would scoop it with her fingers just to make us laugh.

She was so concerned about others that at one point, she asked everybody to clear out of the room, and she wanted only me to stay. She sat with me just one week before she passed and planned out her entire funeral. She went as far as to plan the music, who would speak, and how it would end. She chose an upbeat song, "Shine," by the Newsboys, so when people left, they would feel happy. The service was so packed, they had to put people in the parking lot with speakers to hear the service. Several people came to know Jesus that day. Even in death, she brought the joy of the Lord to others. She was a real hero of the faith.

I do not know how you handle hard times in your life, but I can only strive to handle life with the joy that Haley was able to. I believe she was able to do this because even at the age of seventeen, she had matured and grown into a wonderful, godly woman.

Stop and ask yourself these questions:

- Are you erratic with your emotions?

- Do others shy away from certain topics because of how you may react?

- Are you growing in your relationship with God?

- Are you growing in your relationships with others?

Take a moment and reflect on how you may or may not be growing. Make a decision and commit to growing in the good work Christ is doing in you. Stop right now and pray to God and ask Him for guidance and vision in this area of your life.

CHAPTER 9

Building Upward

—⟋⟍—

That is why it was called Babel—because there the
LORD confused the language of the whole world.
From there the LORD scattered them over the face
of the whole earth.

Genesis 11:9

Tower of Babel

Proverbs 18:10 says, "The name of the LORD is a strong
tower; the righteous run to it and are safe."

In Genesis 11, we read an interesting story of a people
who decided to build. This may sound good in theory. It was
a whole community building together, working in harmony,
and all for a common good. The problem with this particular
community is that they were building for their own glory.
According to verse four, they wanted to build a tower that
would reach heaven to make a "name for themselves."

I think every believer has this same potential, and we
need to be very careful of how we build. Every person has
the potential to grow in knowledge, skill, and power for their
own purpose. I have gotten to the point where it is very hard

for me to watch a few of the television evangelists. It seems that some of these evangelists have taken the opportunity to make their programs more about them than God.

Professional sports are another venue where self has taken over the celebration of the sport. At one time, an athlete did not celebrate until he had actually accomplished something, and then it was a moderate celebration. Now it seems that a first down in football, a single in baseball, or a nice shot in basketball is a cause to draw any and all attention to oneself. Similarly, we have taken over the celebration of what God has done by promoting ourselves in this life.

We need to be a community that is aware of our need to self promote and aim to align our lives that they may promote and bring glory to God alone. I have taught myself to ask myself a question before every endeavor, response, or action. I ask myself, "How can I bring glory to God with . . ." It sounds simple in thought, but just try to stop yourself from doing something and actually ask yourself that question. It is very hard.

It is very hard to not want to edify the flesh of man. We want to bring pleasure to ourselves through the justification of our actions. Inside every one of us there is this desire to win the conflict, to receive justification, to get vengeance, or simply to satisfy the lust of the heart. If we can build our tower to glorify God and not self or man, then we are on our way to growth that will not only glorify God, but also allow others to see God in all situations we encounter.

The problem that the people building the tower had was that the heart had the incorrect motives. Their hearts were motivated to bring attention and glory to themselves. Our hearts are no different today. We need to re-focus our hearts to the things of God. If we realize that we need to bring attention and honor to God rather than man, we start to see each situation in its true context. We start to see the issue as an opportunity and not a burden. We can actually start to understand that for every choice, action, and reaction, there are consequences.

Those consequences can either bring a positive or a negative effect. In the story of the tower, the consequences were too much to overcome. The people could not communicate and had to separate from each other. Sounds like a lot of relationships today. When we refuse to honor God with our lives, we build upon the wrong foundation. If we are not bringing the honor, praise, and glory to God, we must be bringing those avenues to ourselves and Satan.

The way I see life is we are either following or building upon Christ, or we are following or building upon the "evil one." I would never admit that I am glorifying Satan. Even if I knew the choice was not glorifying God, I could not bring myself to admit that. That is why I must ask myself before I make a decision or react to something, "How can I bring glory to God?"

This is why we must build upward. The community building the tower had the right idea, just the wrong motive. We must continually build upward toward God. We must bring Him honor in our whole life. Our life at the moment as well as our long-term plans must bring the attention and honor to Christ. You may ask how we can get started in doing this.

I believe we have to stop being infants. When we accept Christ, we are new to the understanding of what He has done in us. We cannot stay children in our spiritual maturity. We have to make a decision to move from milk to solid food.

From Milk to Solid Food

Hebrews 5:14 says, "But solid food is for the mature, who by constant use have trained themselves to distinguish good from evil."

When my son was an infant, I would get him out of the crib and feed him his bottle. I really enjoyed those times with him. He relied upon me and would just watch me with his big, beautiful eyes while he was eating. It would not be long before he would simply drift off to sleep in my arms. If it was a really good day, I would lay him on my chest and nap with him for a while.

Then one day, without warning, my son grew way past those days. He decided he no longer wanted me to hold him and feed him. He has even decided he does not want milk. He may want water, soda, juice, or fruit punch. He does not want the baby food any longer. No, he wants pizza, chicken nuggets, or a hot dog. He is maturing and has his own opinions on what he may need to eat, or wear, or sleep with; what story he wants to read; or what song he wants to sing. He even makes up his own stories now and tells them to us before bedtime.

Something is happening to my son and my daughter. They are growing up, and I cannot stop this process. Unfortunately, we are not like this spiritually. So many of us come to the Lord and never grow up in Christ. Hebrews 5:13 tells us, "Anyone who lives on milk, being still an infant, is not acquainted with the teaching about righteousness." We need to move from the moment of salvation and start preparing ourselves to be a servant of Christ.

Christ Himself told us, "just as the Son of Man did not come to be served, but to serve, and to give his life as a ransom for many" (Matthew 20:28). So we are made for service as well. We are to become a part of the body of Christ. We are to be used as the hands and feet of Jesus upon this world. Our churches are full of highly qualified and gifted people, people who have abilities and talents, people who have passions and desires, people who have resources and knowledge that no one else can possess. The problem becomes that not many of these people see themselves as servants.

It is truly sad when only 10 percent of the church is doing 100 percent of the work. The only way to get past this is for the church family to wake up and make serving Christ and man their passion. We are told in 1 Peter 4:10, "Each of you should use whatever gift you have received to serve others, as faithful stewards of God's grace in its various forms." This is really good news!

This information from Peter allows us to understand that every type of service, with proper motivation and direction, can and will glorify God. We can move from knowledge of our salvation to active salvation when we realize that we can serve with the qualities and talents that God has given us through our salvation. This, again, is "working out our salvation." We are maturing our salvation by exercising it.

It is amazing to me how many songs a person can memorize. I get the opportunity to ride with people in their cars from time to time. People can sing every verse, song after song. They sing with a passion. They sing with joy and emotion. I can have that same person, whose mind is obviously able to retain lyrics, and ask him to memorize one Scripture, and he just won't do it.

Notice I said "won't." I said this because I know he has the ability to memorize. It seems to me that this comes down to a desire area. We need to set our hearts to grow in Christ. We can only grow and mature in Christ when we allow our hearts to be set upon the things of Christ. When we choose to study His Word, we can grow. When we choose to spend time in prayer, we can grow. When we choose to serve others in Christ, we can grow. When we choose to learn about our faith so we can defend and lead others to Christ, we can grow.

Each of these areas of growth requires us to choose to grow. Unlike my son outgrowing milk bottles, we do have a choice. My son physically grew to a point where he needed more nutrients for human survival. He knew this and wanted to move on. His body told him he needed something more than a liquid diet.

Our soul speaks to us in the same manner. We may call it the valley or a dry spell. It is the time when we no longer "feel" God moving in our lives. We have become stagnant or stale. It is our spirit telling us that we need something more than spiritual milk. It is our soul crying out for the spiritual nutrients that it needs to survive. Our soul, because of the indwelling of the Holy Spirit, has the knowledge of what it needs to be able to fulfill what Christ is setting us apart to do.

Can you imagine what would happen in America if each Christian would choose to listen to the Spirit? Can you see what would happen if each of us would strive to mature in Christ? Wouldn't it be awesome if each of us would really want to become all we could be in Christ? The world could not handle millions of mature people serving Christ.

I believe that the world would be changed forever. I believe that the next generation would have a wonderful benchmark set for them. I believe that we would truly become "one nation under God" again. I cannot imagine if a child would never grow. I look forward to how my own children grow every day. I enjoy seeing the legs get longer, the pants get shorter, and the laughs get louder. I love the way their minds perceive and conceive more every day.

I love the way God has designed us and how that physical design reflects our spiritual design. We need to desire to move from acceptance to service. In the next chapter, we will discuss how to build others through two very different areas. Before we go there, I want you to stop for a moment. I want you to consider where you are in your spiritual maturity. I am going to list a few "benchmarks" for you to consider:

* Do you spend daily time in God's Word?

* Do you spend daily time in prayer with God?

* Do you serve God and man?

* Do you desire to grow up in Christ?

Take a moment and ponder these very simple questions. As you review and think about these questions, ask God to reveal to you where you are not growing, and ask Him for guidance and passion in these areas. I also want to remind you that I am praying for you and for your success to truly live a great life in Christ.

CHAPTER 10

Building Others

—⟋𝔪⟍—

". . . to equip his people for works of service, so that
the body of Christ may be built up . . ."

Ephesians 4:12

I remember when I was playing football in high school. It
was my sophomore year, and we just instituted soccer as
a sport in our school. The football coaches didn't want any
of their players to go out for soccer. My biology teacher was
the new soccer coach. He had just moved from Kentucky
and didn't have the concept of Texas football. In class one
day, he asked me to come out for the soccer team. I really
liked this guy, but I was afraid of how the football coaches
would react.

It had been a while since I played soccer, and I was unsure
of how I would do. I told my teacher this. He assured me he
would handle everything. I went out for the team and made it
as the keeper (goalie). He worked so hard with me. He would
teach me angles and moves. He would teach me the game as
I never knew it, but most of all, he taught me confidence.
When the game was close or on the line, he would simply

comfort me and let me know that no matter the outcome, I could grow from the experience.

He really built me up both in and out of the classroom. He was a great coach, and now as an adult, he is an even better friend.

Being a Coach

Psalm 199:35 says, "Direct me in the path of your commands, for there I find delight."

Coach Baker was a great coach, and inside every one of us is a coach as well. There will always be people who come to you in some way to be coached. Maybe it is a child who comes to you for help. Maybe it will be a sibling seeking advice. Maybe it will be a coworker looking for knowledge. It may be a stranger who just simply needs direction. There will be a time in our lives when we will have the opportunity, no matter how long or short, to coach someone.

I had the opportunity to coach my son in his very first sport. He chose to play soccer on a team of kids four to six years of age. I found out it was like herding cats. Kids were running everywhere. I would hold their hands as they played the game. I would encourage them as they didn't want to go on the field. I felt as if I was in constant chaos. I found out toward the end of the season that I was coaching more than a game. I found out there were life lessons being learned. One child came out of her shell and really enjoyed the game. Another boy learned confidence, while another learned he could be loved.

The biggest lesson that was learned was learned by me. I learned I could be coached as well. I listened to the supportive comments by parents, I had an assistant coach that was a backbone and a wonderful support tool, and I was coached in the art of love by the kids on the team.

Coaching is not about knowing the answers. No, coaching someone is helping them find the answers. Coaching, in my experience, means knowing where to send others for the answers. We must be able to listen to people and truly try to identify with them. Once we really listen, we can direct them to the Bible and prayer for the start of discovery. If we do not know where it is in the Bible, then we can admit that and help them search.

Coaching is not counseling. We are not fixing the person, but rather we are guiding them to the truth. We are not telling them the answers; we are helping them find the answers. They are being built up by the support of a caring person, and they are gaining maturity and knowledge in the Word. There is nothing more enjoyable than seeing someone when they "get it." There is that moment when the bulb comes on and they see the truth clearly.

Coaching and mentoring can almost be exchangeable here. The art of mentoring is almost a lost practice in the Christian community today. We want to teach classes, which are needed, and preach, which is a must, but to take our own time and actually take a new Christian under our wing is almost unthinkable. There was a time when a new Christian came into the fellowship and someone was designated to that individual.

They would have them in their home, eat with them, read the Word with them, and pray with them. If you would just seek out one babe in Christ and invest into his life, I believe you would be amazed at the fruit and impact that one life would have on the world and you. We have become such an antisocial America. We have moved our grills to fenced-in backyards. We have made the living room smaller and each bedroom bigger in our homes. We have multiple computers, televisions, and cell phones in our families. We have become a society that invites isolation.

We need to become a community where we contribute to the whole, where we help our neighbor and extend a hand. We need to become a community where we invite people into our homes, share the good news, and encourage them to grow. Become a coach, a mentor, a friend in Christ.

Being a Friend

John 15:13 says, "Greater love has no one than this, that he lay down his life for his friends."

Being a true friend brings us to another area of building others. I want to talk about family relationships, if I may. There are way too many parents of young children who are too busy trying to be a friend instead of a parent. I know we all want to be liked by our children; I know I do. I also know what my children need: They need a father who will set the example of what a Christian dad is. They need guidelines and parameters to provide protection. They need my love as a father to support and encourage them through this life.

The last thing my child needs is me as a friend who will agree with them and allow them to do as they please so I can avoid conflict. Let me give you an example: When my children were infants, I could not stand to hear them lie in their crib and cry. It tore me up inside. I would beg my wife, "Please let me go pick her up." Cami would tell me that we could not do this. She explained that by not getting them out of bed, we were teaching them to set sleeping times and teaching them the discipline that they could not get what they wanted by just crying.

This was a very hard lesson for me to learn. However, after a few weeks of this torture, I found that my infant actually learned these lessons. I learned that as she grew into a toddler, she would actually ask to go to nap time. I could not believe that this actually worked. I have found the same principle works in life relationships. When you give people what they need and not what they want, they eventually understand that you have their best interest in mind.

When you do this, they begin to respect the friendship and value you as a person. The friendship relationship has to be built upon honest, genuine concern for the other person. This produces an authentic relationship where each person can be built up to be all they can be. When you share with a person what the Word says and pray with them, you have laid the relationship on God's sure foundation.

We need to be willing to risk pleasing people and allow the friendship to exhibit the love of the truth in their lives. The Bible is very clear that our "yes be yes, and our no be no." We cannot build people's faith by being unclear with the gospel. To allow ourselves, and others, to live truly great lives in Christ, we must be clear about the Christian life. We have an obligation to build up and protect our brothers in Christ as well.

There were many who came before us who gave their lives up for the gospel. They did this not for the moment, but that we may have the Word available to us today. There are people today giving their lives up for the cause of Christ. In America, we are not asked to do that. I am not asking you to do that. I am asking you to allow your fears and pride to be martyred for the cause. Put away what may happen, and allow yourself to be used by God to build up another person in Christ.

Husbands and Wives

1 Corinthians 7:16 says, "How do you know, wife, whether you will save your husband? Or, how do you know, husband, whether you will save your wife?"

I want to take a moment and speak to those of you who are married or will be one day. I have found one of the best ways to build up my partner is to do two very simple things.

I have found that by praying out loud with my wife, we have opened a whole new dimension in our communication. When I, on a daily basis, share with God what is really going on in my life, with my wife there listening, there does not seem to be anything we cannot talk about. When I tell God how much she means to me, what I need from her, what wonderful qualities He gave her, and so on, I find that we can open up to each other as well.

I have found it makes it easier for me to speak with others as well because I am learning to be authentic in my prayer life. She is right there, and I am accountable to her, as well as God, because she has heard me talk to God. Because I have learned this freedom, I am able to communicate with others more openly and honestly.

I have also found that I am not as nervous to bring up uncomfortable subjects because I have poured my heart out before God while she listened. She does the same, and it has been such a blessing to hear my wife speak to God. To allow me to be a part of hearing her talk to her first love brings a joy that I cannot describe. This time of prayer brings us closer to each other, and what was uncomfortable to begin with has become something I long for.

This was not always so comfortable. When we were dating, it was very difficult. I always wanted to impress her with my life. To expose my weaknesses to her would violate every "code of the man" I had ever followed. I could pray in front of hundreds of people at a worship service, but I could not expose my prayer life to her. The first few times, my prayers were very superficial. After some time, I began to open my heart before her and God. It was such a liberating experience, and it's crucial to our spiritual life today.

The second thing Cami and I do to build each other in Christ is read together. Whether we are reading the Bible, a devotional, or a book together, we have found that reading aloud and sharing with each other allows us to learn better and understand each other's passions more, and it lays a foundation for communication. Many times after we read, we will share thoughts of what has been read. It sparks some wonderful conversations and ideas for our family.

Reading together also has made me more comfortable reading with my children. I have become more confident in my reading and in the reading of bedtime books with my kids. I have found that reading together has enlightened my time with my family.

Now let me allow you in on something. I am not a great reader or speaker. I was so intimidated by reading out loud with Cami when we were dating. I hated to hear my voice out loud like that. I was embarrassed to read. I am not a great reader. I was worried about writing this book, for I had never really written like this before. The only way I am able to do any of these things now is I have been built up in Christ with the help of a loving friend, wife, and family.

Christ knows what each of us needs in order to grow. If we say yes to the opportunities He presents to us, He will grow us. Listen to Him, and be willing to step out into new territories. I want to have you think for just a moment about how you are building the people in your lives:

- Are you reaching out to them with the truth?

- Are you willing to mentor them?

- Are you willing to risk stepping out of your comfort zone and into the unknown with them and Christ?

Take a moment and pray about these issues, and ask Christ to give you the understanding and courage to do His will.

CHAPTER 11

Send

—〜〜—

Therefore go.
Matthew 28:19a

A painter does not purchase the paint and then not use the paint. He will not set up the easel and canvas and never create the masterpiece that is upon his heart. No, a painter will carefully pick out his supplies and then, with careful thought, start to apply the brush strokes until the painting is mature and complete.

This same painter also will make available the painting to others that they may be blessed by its beauty. The artist may display the painting in a museum or gallery. He may auction the painting or sell it so it may grace the wall of someone's home or office. However the artist displays his art, he is in anticipation that someone else may benefit from the beauty of the art.

This same artist had to work at his trade to become an artist who can peddle his trade. I am sure his art style, ability, and beauty has changed over the time of practice, frustration and futility. The artist noticed that there was something that drew him to painting, and now he wants to use that tool for others to enjoy.

Sending Yourself

Acts 22:21 says, "Then the Lord said to me, 'Go; I will send you far away to the Gentiles.' "

It was summer, and I was fourteen years of age. I was walking through a bayou— maybe it was a big ditch— gigging frogs. Yes, gigging frogs with a two-pronged stick. I was singing the hymn "There's Just Something About That Name." I sat down for a moment and thanked God for the wonderful day. As I tried to get back up, it was as if there was a hand upon my forehead. I could not get up! It was at that moment I heard the tug of the Holy Spirit on my heart to go into the ministry.

I wrestled with God on this thought for a while, but I still could not stand. Once I finally agreed with God that I would follow Him into the ministry, I was immediately able to stand. It took a long time for me to finally go into the ministry, but I did start doing small things. I started to assist the local Little League football teams. I did puppets at my church. I did what I thought I could do at my young age.

I finally came to the point, several years later, when I had to decide to quit the job I was in and go into the ministry full time. I have never looked back. Things have not always been easy, but things have always been right. There is a saying, "If I do what is right, God will do what is best."

God is calling every one of us to something. Maybe it is in the church as a lay leader; maybe it is in our community as a volunteer. God can call us to too many areas to try to list here. The area is not important to discuss as much as the willingness to go is.

So many people are afraid that if they say yes to God, they will be saying no to the rest of their lives. I know I was afraid that by saying yes to God, I would end up in a third-world country digging ditches for the Lord! It seems to be a common fear among believers.

We seem to be so worried that God does not know what we really need. God will place you where He needs you. He will place you there for the duration He needs you there. You will accomplish only what He wants to accomplish during your service. The thing we have to understand is that He is in total control. All we have to be is willing.

God will not call us to anything He will not equip us for. Moses gave excuse after excuse as to why he was not worthy of the task God had given him. He knew as a human, he was not equipped to free an entire nation from the grips of a headstrong ruler. He was looking for every way out that he could think of. God called Moses, and God equipped Moses.

Moses did not make the "Hall of Faith" because he was super human. No, Moses made it to the "Hall of Faith" because he was willing. We may never be called to such a task as Moses, but we may be called to such a task as the young boy and the loaves and fishes.

In John 6, we read about a young boy who was willing. All he had was five small barley loaves of bread and two small fish. The small boy could have kept his lunch, but he was willing to give it away and say yes to Jesus Christ. I know it doesn't seem as if the boy did much, but he really did.

You see, he could have said, "This is mine, and it is all I have." He could have said, "I am bringing this home, and my mother is expecting all of it."

Instead, he was simply willing to give it all to Jesus and allow Jesus to use it as He saw fit. Jesus did use this, and about five thousand people were fed by what a small child gave that day. Each of us has been called to serve. If you have accepted Christ, you have been called. You may be called to work quietly behind the scenes, or you may serve right up front for everyone to see.

The place of calling is really irrelevant. The willingness to go and obey is what matters. Abraham was willing to leave his homeland, Elijah was willing to take on four hundred fifty priests of a false religion, and David was willing to take on a giant of a man. What are you willing to do for the Lord of all creation?

What are you willing to do for the One Who laid His life down for you? He has given you promises that He will provide for, protect, and care for you. The only requirement for you is to be willing. To be willing simply means you have to trust in the One Who called you. When Jesus walked this earth, just His presence must have had a profound effect on people. We can read the stories of how they left everything to follow Him. They left their jobs, homes, families, money, and material possessions to simply follow a man they just met.

We are in a much better position. We have read the stories in His Word. We have seen His work played out in the generations that have come before us. We know that He provides and supplies all of our needs. Yet, there is this still small, voice that can convince us to refrain from saying yes. I do not know what He is calling you to do. I do not know what experience lies ahead in your life. I do know that Jesus has a purpose for every believer, and to fulfill that purpose, we must be willing to say yes to Christ and no to our own desires.

When I was called to the church I serve, I did not immediately want to come. You see, I had an offer from a much larger church in a much bigger city with a much better ability for pay. I had friends telling me that my career would die if I chose to come to this little church instead of the nice church with a better offer. My wife and I began to really seek the Lord and what He wanted from us.

After much prayer and seeking God, we had an incredible peace about going to the smaller church. The bigger church was very nice; God touched their hearts as well. But looking back, we now see why God wanted us here. We could never be as happy serving as where we are right now. God has blessed us in so many ways, and we have created authentic relationships that I could never have imagined could exist.

To be sent out, we have to be willing to go. We also have another factor we must consider while serving Christ, and that is we must send out others.

Sending Out Others

2 Corinthians 13:13 says, "All the saints send their greetings."

Missionaries, pastors, teachers, leaders, elders, deacons, and many other positions in the church seem to be what I thought of when I thought about people being sent out to do the Lord's work. I never seemed to think of mothers, fathers, doctors, firemen, police officers, friends, janitors, and the rest of the people I run into on a daily basis.

I was a volunteer youth leader in a church many years ago when I met Stacey. Stacey was a wonderful youth pastor at the church where I volunteered. Stacey had a way with the kids, and the kids just loved him as well. Stacey pulled me to the side one day and said, "You are making a difference." I could not understand what he was saying. How was I making a difference? I just showed up every week and did what Stacey told me to do.

Stacey explained to me that God was preparing to send me out to do His service in the lives of others and that the impact I could have for God could be tremendous. Now, at the time Stacey told me this, I was working in the insurance industry and not looking at my life in terms of doing ministry. I simply did my duty and volunteered at my local church. Stacey then explained to me that the difference I was making was simply being available—available to *what* was a big question that entered my mind. He went on to help me understand that when I give of my time, it encourages others to do the same.

He also explained that the teens were learning to apply themselves as well. It started to become clearer to me that my being willing to serve could encourage others to serve as well.

We have a desire not only to succeed in life ourselves, but to see others succeed as well. If you think about this, you will see that you like to see others succeed. When I watch an athletic event, I want to see someone do something rather spectacular. I love a close game at the end of regulation. I love to see someone win at the last moment. I like to see someone when they pass a test or accomplish a goal.

There is joy when we see others succeed. The truly great part of seeing others succeed is when we get to play a part in this. I have numerous letters from people who once were teenagers under my care in a youth group. Some of these young adults were not going down a path to any type of success. I would never tell anyone what to do in life, but through biblical encouragement and support, I have seen many of these young adults very excited where they have ended up.

Some are parents now; others are in the professional world, and still others have decided to go into some type of full-time ministry. Every one of these kids is very excited about the decisions he has made. The area that the kids seem most excited about is where they are serving the Lord. Some may be volunteering at the local church, while others are working in their communities. All seem so happy to see that they are serving.

Every believer who comes into our lives has been given a gift from God. Most of these individuals have been given more than one gift. If we can encourage each believer to use his gifts to glorify God and to inspire others to believe in Christ, the kingdom is going to multiply, and millions of people can find the truth. There is a great joy in seeing others begin to use their gifts and the joy that accompanies. People working in their gifts seem to enjoy their service more, they seem to be more productive, and they seem to have an approach to life that brings joy to others.

I was happy working in the insurance industry before I went into the ministry. I was paid well, treated well, and respected by my colleagues. I went to work excited about my job each day. That is what it was, a job. I went to a job each day and was not fulfilled in my life. When I started to volunteer in the teen group at my local church, I began to have something that I looked forward to each day. Whether I was planning an event, spending time encouraging a child, or getting my hands dirty working for the community, I was experiencing something I had never felt.

When we start to spend time with a person, we start to see the unique way that God can use him. We start seeing the things he really cares about and the things that do not seem to interest him at all. When we see those things that seem to bring a sparkle to his eye, we should encourage him to seek the Lord and ask if he is being led to find a way to get involved in those areas for which he has a passion.

When God equips us in an area, He also gives us a desire to work in that area. We should never become so blind that we think the ministries for Christ exist only as they are in the local church. No, if someone in our church community has a passion and giftedness in an area, we should want to encourage them to branch out into those areas.

We have a gentleman in our church that has a passion to help those who are a little less fortunate. They may need a small appliance repaired or a lawn serviced. He really has a passion for these people, and God has gifted him to know how to do many things in the repair and labor fields. Because of this passion and skill, we have created a whole new ministry to our community. Many other people who are gifted in these areas as well have signed on to be a part of this ministry.

When we give people the opportunity to serve in the areas in which God has gifted them, there is no end to what God can and will do through them. I also feel we should start as early on in people's lives as we can. When people come to Christ, we need to start looking for areas for which they have passions. A lot of times God will elevate their talents into full-blown gifts. Someone may have a passion to paint, but once he has committed his life to Christ, the passion and talent move to a level above his natural ability.

If we truly want to build the kingdom of Christ, we need to allow people to be truly all that God has designed them to be. I am not into certain types of music. However, I have come to the conclusion that even the music style I cannot relate to is exactly what someone else may need to hear to connect with God at times. I am so proud of the church where I serve. We have several different praise teams in our worship service rotation. The styles differ from very traditional, to praise music, to bluegrass, to contemporary. We have really tapped into allowing each believer to use his gift and passion to convey the Word of God in song.

I am also looking at the qualities and passions that God has given my children. I watch their likes and dislikes, their loves and hates. I want to encourage them to be all they can be for the kingdom of Christ. If I really want to encourage them, I need to know where to encourage them. I want to see my children serve wonderful, godly lives on this earth and to be all they can be for Christ. This means I have to invest in them and their gifts.

I want to encourage you to never look past what someone has a passion for. It may not be your thing or your joy, but it may very well be what that person is being called to by God. You do not have to understand it, have knowledge of it, or even like it, but you can encourage him to be everything he can be for Christ in it.

Gifts for His Time

Romans 12:6 says, "We have different gifts, according to the grace given to each of us."

Grace is such a wonderful understanding. According to the New Webster's Dictionary and Thesaurus of the English Language, Grace is "unconstrained and undeserved divine favor or goodwill." We do not deserve grace, and we do not deserve the gifts we are given by God as well. We are, however, given gifts. We are given these gifts according to what God wants to impart upon each of us. I want you to understand that as you mature in Christ and grow in service, your gifts may change as well.

There are many different stages to a physical life. To name a few, there is infancy, toddler years, childhood, adolescence, and young adulthood, adulthood, middle age years, and senior adulthood. Many stages of the physical life exhibit many different stages of physical abilities. I may go from crawling to walking, from walking to running, and from running to simply walking again. As I mature physically, my body allows me to do things differently.

As a spiritual body, I may be allowed to see my gifts mature or even change over a lifetime. I may find that I have a heart to care for people. I may start out by simply being there to listen to those who need a friendly person to lean on. This gift and passion may grow into a life of a full-time counselor. Maybe because you care for people, the gift changes to an area of helping others. Instead of just listening, you start to physically help make things happen for them. Maybe they cannot go to the store on their own, so you start to do the shopping for them. Maybe you become a caretaker.

At different times in our lives, we are given different abilities and gifts to accomplish what God wants done at that time. Years ago, I took some teens to Mexico on a missions trip. I do not speak Spanish. The leader we met in Mexico gave me the job of going door to door to notify the residents that there would be a drama in the streets in fifteen minutes. I had no idea how this was to be accomplished. I prayed,

"Lord, give me a way to communicate this information so these people can hear your Word."

I knocked on the first door. It was more like a piece of steel laid over an opening where a door should be. A woman came to the opening and handed me her infant baby girl. She asked me, "What are you here for?" I actually understood her! I opened my mouth, and I was speaking Spanish! God had gifted me at that moment with a tongue I did not speak to communicate what He wanted to be said.

I handed her baby back to her, I thanked her, and I went to many other doors to pass the news along. More than two hundred people came to the streets, and many of them accepted Christ that day. I was able to speak the whole trip in Spanish to those people. I preached the Word in their native language, and God's kingdom was increased that week. When I left there, so did my ability to speak Spanish. God has a time and place for everything, even His gifts He gives us.

Stop a moment and think about your life right now. Think about what God is doing around you and how you can be involved. Think about the gifts, passions and abilities He has granted to you and how these things can be used to build His kingdom. What is He really putting upon your heart? Understand it may be for the time as it is now, or it may be building you for a later time in your life.

Take just a moment to understand your gifts more. I want to encourage you to ask yourself a couple of questions:

- Do you trust God with the gifts that He has given to you?

- Are you willing to step out of your comfort zone and serve Him with your gifts?

- Is there someone you can encourage in his gifts and passions?

- Am I open to the fact that God can use me for such a time as this?

- Am I willing to be used for what God wants in the lives of others?

Take a moment and pray how God can better use you to encourage others in your life. Remember, I am praying for you as well.

CHAPTER 12

Your Gifts for Others

—⚍—

Each of you should use whatever gift you have received to serve others, as faithful stewards of God's grace in its various forms.

1 Peter 4:10

Serving others is not a popular statement to be made in our self-serving society. America is a society that wants to be served. We have drive-through fast food, drive-through banks, even drive-through wedding chapels. We have people who can do our nails, hair, face, and feet. We want to be served, and we want it now! We look at somebody serving us as someone beneath us. These people may have jobs that pay less than others, or we just see them as those who serve us. I want to tell you about true service for others.

Jesus was the most gifted teacher this world has or will ever see. He was superior in His knowledge. He was advanced in His ability to speak. He was able to control His tongue when others could not. He had a following that would make any power seeker envious. Yet, we read in John 13 that Jesus became the servant to teach a lesson. He took on the role of the lowest servant to wash each of the disciples' feet.

This was a true lesson for these men to learn. You see, the streets of Jesus' time were not like our own. These streets consisted of dirt, mud, animal droppings, and even the sewage for the city at times. Your feet would be contaminated with bacteria, disease, filth, smell, and many other things we will not go into. Jesus was a Master to these men. It would have been an honor for any of them to be picked to wash Jesus' feet.

Jesus became the least to do the most. He used this illustrated teaching method to bring these men to understand how important it would be for them to become servants themselves.

My first pastor I worked for had a philosophy. He felt that if someone came to him and wanted to work in the ministry that he would test them. He would allow them to come to the program they desired to work in and then would give them only one duty: the duty of cleaning up after everyone else. If they could do this for a certain period of time—he never told them how long or why they were doing it—with joy and love, then he felt he had found a good candidate for ministry.

Sounds kind of harsh, but it really seemed to have worked. I, after cleaning up after teenagers for a couple of years, am still in the ministry and love serving those in my flock. But to serve takes more than being willing. To serve, we have to understand the grace we must impart upon others.

Jesus gave this lesson, as my pastor had given me, to show them that we must love those God has entrusted to us. God has given us abilities that we would not possess without His touch, and we are to show others the same grace that God is showing us.

I was a volunteer youth leader, and I was still working full time in the insurance industry. I had to go to a body shop to inspect a damaged vehicle. This particular establishment was located in a very rough neighborhood. It was known for a lot of gang activity. I arrived and went through the open gates. Once I was there, I exited my vehicle, only to find the business was closed. I turned to get back in my car when I noticed a group of young men standing at the gates.

These young men were not the type of young men I wanted to be around. They wore baggy clothes. They wore bandanas in their back pockets. They chose to wear their hats setting sideways on their heads. They were very intimidating, and I had my own preconceived notions about this "type" of person. I had no desire to serve these young men. I only had a desire to get as far away from them as I could.

These men started hurling insults and slurs at me. I have to admit, I was really scared, and I wanted to bolt out of there. I had a couple of choices: I could get in my car and speed at them and pray I did not hit one of them, or I could simply wait it out and see what happened. I chose to wait it out. I sat on the trunk of my car, and they started to approach me. I had no idea what to do. Do I give them my wallet and ask them not to hurt me? Do I try to attack them before they attack me? I was so lost at this point.

What did I do? I sat there not knowing what to do, that is what I did. They started to poke my chest and push me a little.

Finally, one of them said, "Say something."

I did. I said, "Uh, I love you."

You should have seen the look on each of their faces. I had no idea where that came from. I just knew that I was really going to die now!

The next thing that was said really shocked me.

The young man said, "Why?"

I took the opportunity to tell them about God's love and grace and how, because of His love toward me, I have a love toward them. (I do not know how much I loved them at the time, but I did find out much later.) Two of those boys accepted Christ right there, and they told me I had safe passage anytime I wanted to come into their hood. God took a talent to speak and turned it into a gift to reach those two young men at that particular moment in life.

After that day, I would stop in and see them and speak with them. Not all of them accepted or believed, but they were all willing to listen. I became a servant to those boys. They had my number and would call me when they were in trouble or had a problem. God allowed them to see His gifts in me and not what they were used to seeing in people. They saw the gift of love.

Our churches today need people to be willing to serve in their gifts. We need to reach out to the hurting and lost. It seems that so many churches leave all of the service to the minister or to the few who do volunteer. When we can see that every believer has a gift to offer to others, and encourage them to serve others, we will be totally shocked at what the church can do.

We need men and women who will dedicate their lives to Christ, not just in theory, but to be lived out each day. Think about it. How many people do we drive past each day who are having car trouble? Do we even think about stopping any longer? What about that neighbor who is sick? Do we think about cutting his lawn? What about that friend who has lost his job? Do we invite him over and cook meals for him?

It seems we have become so desensitized that we do not even notice the hurting or needy on a daily basis. Jesus said, "It is not the healthy who need a doctor, but the sick" (Matthew 9:12). We seem to have lost sight that we are to be Christ-like. To be Christ-like, we must imitate Christ. He came to help the needy, and each of us was a needy person at one time. We were lost, and He gave us His gift of grace.

If we could look at life with the backdrop of grace, we could see others more clearly. Just to understand that Christ loved us enough to impart His gift upon us should be enough to motivate us to want to reach others with the gifts God has given us.

I want to bring you to a place right now for you to examine how you view others. Do you expect others to serve you—not in the way of a master to a slave, but in the way of people bringing you glory? Maybe you expect to be waited on instead of you doing the waiting on others. Maybe you expect everyone to notice your accomplishments, and you never encourage others. I am not sure how you see your life, but do take a moment and reflect on your daily life in Christ.

If you see any area where you need to engage your gifts for the benefit of others, I want you to ask God to lead you right now in that knowledge. Ask His Holy Spirit to guide you down the path to impart your gifts on others. This may be done through a program at your church, or it may be an individual effort. Whatever it may be, do not allow the joy of service in your gifts pass you by.

I encourage you to really seek the answers to the following questions:

- Can you see yourself as a servant to those you look down upon?

- Will you seek out someone to bless with your gifts?

- Can you serve someone and not seek out gratitude for your service?

You may not receive the recognition, fame, or headlines for serving others upon this earth, but know, "And without faith it is impossible to please God, because anyone who comes to him must believe that he exists and that he rewards those who earnestly seek him" (Hebrews 11:6).

CHAPTER 13

Encouragement for You and Others

—ᗢ—

Surely I am with you always.
Matthew 28:20

It had been a lousy day. I went into the church at six in the morning to help open the school. I got hit by two complaints before eight in the morning. By lunchtime, I had to handle two disciplinary actions on two students I really liked and respected. I had a soccer game to coach, and we got killed. I went home, and at twelve-thirty in the morning, my phone rang. It was a mother of one of the teens in the youth group.

She had stated that her daughter had been out all night, and she believed she was in a crack house. I got out of bed and went to the address given. The front door was open, so I went in. She was sitting on the couch with a couple of older guys. I took her by the hand and started to walk to the door. As I put her in her seat, I heard a loud "pop." I turned to see a man with a pistol pointed right at us. I hurried to the driver's seat and floored it.

I stopped sometime later at a gas station, and in the windshield right in front of where she was sitting was a bullet mark. I stopped right there and thanked God for being with us during that moment. I thanked God for keeping that bullet from penetrating the windshield. After I stopped shaking, I took her home, and her mother eventually got her help for her problem.

Life is going to throw you twists and fears whenever it can. The one great encouragement is that God is always with us. No matter what is going on, He will never leave us alone. He has made this a promise. As a matter of fact, you can see through the different illustrations in this book that I was never alone. We do go through times when we are in the valley.

The valley is a very lonely place for us to be. We were made for relationships, and when the one relationship that gave us the very heart that beats in us seems so far away, we can become very lonely. Jesus understood this all too well. When Christ was upon the cross, He asked this question of God: About three in the afternoon Jesus cried out in a loud voice, "Eli, Eli, lema sabachthani?" (which means "My God, my God, why have You forsaken me?") (Matthew 27:46). For just a moment, the pain, anguish, sadness, and stillness of the cross had Jesus in the valley. For just that moment, He felt all alone. The people of the earth had rejected Him, the disciples had fled from Him, and His Father seemed so far away.

We all go through valleys. We all have moments when God seems so far away from our lives. We pray but feel nothing. We sing songs but find no comfort. We read the Bible and do not understand what it is saying to us. We all have valleys. The best news is that God is not based on what we are feeling.

God is always with us, and whether we feel Him or not, He is still there. We have to come to a point of trust in Christ that no matter how we feel or how big the circumstance, we are not alone. He is there! Jesus made a decision just a few moments later when He allowed Himself to die upon the cross. He had the power to call down the angels from heaven to take Him off the cross. He could have come down and destroyed all of those present at the cross.

But no, He chose to die and do the Father's will for you and for me. He went into the darkness of death knowing that God was with Him. Three days later, He was alive and well and doing His Father's will, and He is still at it to this day.

Each of us comes to a time when we think that God has abandoned us. He has not abandoned us, and maybe, just maybe, we are not the strength that is getting us through it at all. Maybe God has been carrying us the whole time, and we just thought we were doing the work. God has a way that we cannot understand, but when we look back, we can see the hand of God and where it has been in our lives.

In 2005, my family was hit with the news that my brother would be put to death by the state of Texas by lethal injection. This was very hard for us to take. This was very confusing to accept that we could allow this to happen, even though there was nothing we could do. I loved my brother very much, and even though he was in prison, he still was my older brother, and I still listened to his advice and leadership as my older sibling.

When the time grew closer, I grew more misunderstanding of where God was in all of this. That was until I trusted in God. You see, my brother had asked if I would stand in with my parents, my other brother, and a family friend and witness the execution. I had no idea how to handle this. There is a place in every person, deep down somewhere, where we all ask ourselves, "How much is enough." I was at this point. I wanted to be strong for my family and even for my brother. I was beginning to feel weaker with every thought and concern.

The last few years had produced several pains and trials. My son had gone through the staph infection, we had lost my teenage niece, and I had to perform funerals for a couple of men very close to me. I was at a breaking point, and the valley seemed way too deep. God has a way of showing up just in time.

There is a place in Huntsville, Texas, next to the prison that is called The Hospitality House. This is a nonprofit home where families can go before an execution. They allow the person who is to be executed to call this house and spend time speaking with the family members. They provide food, books, prayer, and caring. As I was there in this awful situation, I started to see God in the faces of those caring for my family. They did not get in the way. The people of The Hospitality House were just there. They provided simple things like a smile, a cup of water, or maybe a pat on the back. They cared.

I still didn't know how I would handle the whole situation, but I knew that I had seen God. There is still not a day that I do not think of my brother or that moment at the execution, but God was with us, and God is still getting us through it. He never left us alone, and He is still with us every step of life's way.

I read of Mary and Martha and the loss of their brother, Lazarus. I see how they felt abandoned by Jesus and how Jesus used that valley to bring on a mountain. The Bible is full of wonderful stories of how people felt alone and later found out that God had been there all the time.

I want to remind you that the battle is not fought in the valley. Moses in the Bible was standing on the mountain as the Israelites fought a battle. He remained on the mountain with his arms lifted to heaven. As his hands would lower, the Israelites would begin to lose the battle. When his hands went toward heaven, the Israelites would begin to win the battle. The battle was being fought in the spiritual realms and not in the physical valley. Our battles are not fought in the valley, either. No, our battles are being fought in the spiritual realms as well. Give those valleys to God, and lift your eyes to the One Who can fight all of your battles.

If I may, I want to encourage you to know that God is with you. He has not left you. He will not leave you. If you have accepted Him as your Savior, then He is with you. Sometimes we have to keep plugging along and just know that He is there. Other times we may need to stop and wait on Him to make Himself known. I want to encourage you to know that as a child of God, you have a power so strong that is with you at all times.

No matter what the mountain is that comes your way, you have the Holy Spirit with you every step of the way. When we accept Christ, we are given the Holy Spirit as a Comforter. This Comforter is with us, and we have a source of strength that the world does not have. The world cannot conquer the Spirit, and the world does not have the means or knowledge to defeat our God. Trust in the Lord, and know that He is there and that He will never leave you.

Points of encouragement:

* Know that God is always there.

* Know that you can never separate yourself from God's love (Romans 8:39).

* You are special.

* You were designed for success.

* You have been prayed for.

Take a moment and just thank the Lord for being there. Thank Him for being there when you did not feel Him or see Him. I want to encourage you, just as I saw with the people of The Hospitality House, to look for God to show up when all seems lost. He will not let you down.

CHAPTER 14

Win, Build, and Send for the Kingdom of Christ
(May you live a truly great life in Christ)

—∞—

I have come that they may have life, and have it to
the full.

John 10:10b

I want to thank you for taking the time to read this book. I
pray that you have been encouraged to **win, build, and
send for the kingdom of Christ**. It is not enough to read this
book and then set it aside. It is not enough to know what you
should do but never do it. It is not enough to get a gift and
never open it.

I want you to take what you have learned and use it in your
families, local church, community, workplace, and every-
where you may travel. Let people see that you have been
won from the world by Christ. Allow yourself to encourage
others to come to know Christ as their Savior. Be excited
to grow in your faith and to become all you can become in
Christ. Employ joy so that you also may invest in other lives

with which you may come into contact. I pray that you can build them up in Christ as well.

Then I want you to send. Allow yourself to be sent into the areas of life to minister to those to whom God is directing you. Look for opportunities to send others on their way in Christ. Encourage them in their gifts and passions. Encourage them to step out in faith. Encourage them to become servants to God and man.

Together we can change the world, but it starts one life at a time. It starts with a willing life. It starts with a life that will glorify God in all things. It starts with you.

May God bless your endeavors as you get on the road to the life-changing way of serving others with your gifts, passions, and grace as God has given them to you. Remember that I am praying for you, and I want to hear from you.

Remember to WIN, BUILD, AND SEND for the KINGDOM of CHRIST!

A people without understanding will come to ruin!

Hosea 4:14

In Christ,

Bobby D. Hopper
hopperbc@yahoo.com

Study Guide:
To Win-Build-and Send
Preparing to Live a Truly Great
Life in Christ

—∿—

Study Guide:
To Win-Build-and Send
Preparing to Live a Truly Great
Life in Christ

—ᘑ—

What is Win-Build-Send?

Matthew 28:18-20

Then Jesus came to them and said, "All authority in heaven and on earth has been given to me. Therefore go and make disciples of all nations, baptizing them in the name of the Father and of the Son and of the Holy Spirit, and teaching them to obey everything I have commanded you. And surely I am with you always, to the very end of the age."

—∿—

To understand what Win-Build-and Send is we need to start at the beginning. The beginning is the very start of a person's life. No, I am not speaking of your physical birth; I am speaking of when you truly start to live. Some will say this begins when the kids grow up and move out of the home. Others say it starts when they find true financial freedom. I have heard it said that life begins when we allow ourselves to really begin to live.

1)   **When do you believe that living life to the fullest begins? What is your opinion on when life begins for a human?**

    _____

    _____

    _____

2)   **Have you ever had a moment when you realized you had experienced a life changing moment? Explain that moment and how it impacted your life.**

    _____

    _____

    _____

3)   **Do you believe that God wants you to live life to the fullest?**

    _____

    _____

    _____

4) How do we view "life to the fullest" from a world view? How do we view "life to the fullest" from a Christ-like view?

_____

_____

_____

5) How important is it to have a vision (goals) for your life? List some goals you would like to accomplish in your life.

_____

_____

_____

By applying the concept of the Win-Build-and Send method you can live the Christian life to its fullest and experience all God has in store for you. We are told in Hosea 4:14, "...*a people without understanding will come to ruin!*" We need a clear understanding, a vision, of what we are to do with our Christianity. I pray this small book can lead you in your understanding of how to Win-Build-and Send for the Kingdom of Christ!

May God bless your journey as you Win-Build-and Send for His Kingdom.

Study Guide:
To Win-Build-and Send
Preparing to Live a Truly Great
Life in Christ

(Ch. 1)

—᷍᷍᷍—

To Win

Matthew 28:19 *"Therefore go and make disciples of all nations, baptizing them in the name of the Father and of the Son and of the Holy Spirit"*

I am a guy who loves sports. I grew up in Texas where football was king. I played football, watched football, and even dreamed about football. It was the way of life for a kid in the heart of Texas. I dreamed big dreams as I watched the Houston Oilers play in the Astrodome. I would play in the front yard and fantasize that I was Johnnie Unitas or Roger Staubach. I ended every fantasy with time running out and I would throw the winning touchdown as time expired. I won the Superbowl! What a wonderful life that would have been.

1) **Have you, at some point of your life, ever had a dream of what you really wanted to be?**

_____

_____

_____

2) Have you ever wanted to please others first? How do you gauge success in your life? (How do you seek approval?)

_____

_____

_____

3) What does "God taking the lead" convey to you?

_____

_____

_____

4) Have you ever quit something? What? Why? Does it seem easier to quit than to persevere?

_____

_____

_____

5) Do you see yourself as "designed for greatness"? Why? Why not?

_____

_____

_____

6) Have you ever succeeded only to find yourself still feeling empty?

_____

_____

_____

Joseph the "Winner"
Genesis 37:5 "*Joseph had a dream…*"

Joseph, of the Bible, was a person who had big dreams in life. Joseph dreamed that he would have a very high position and that even his own siblings and parents would be subjective to him and his decisions. Their very life would fall into his hands if be so. Now Joseph had grand dreams of winning in life but it was not without some severe road blocks.

7) **Have you ever dreamed of being something more than you currently are?**

_____

_____

_____

8) **Do you believe that people of any age can be used for great things today?**

_____

_____

_____

9) **Is it possible to be content in very extreme conditions?**

_____

_____

_____

10) **Note some ways in which we change our lives due to the current fashion or fad of our time.**

_____

_____

_____

11) **What would it look like to live in a place where you are viewed by your character and not your looks, status, or power?**

_____

_____

_____

12) When looking at your faith where do you see the foundations of your life truly are grounded in?

_____

_____

_____

Paul: "Counted all as Joy"

Romans 4:8 *"Blessed is the man whose sin the Lord will never count against him."*

Another figure, in the Bible, was the Apostle Paul. Paul was a man who "counted it as pure joy" no matter what circumstance he was in. In 2 Corinthians 11 we read about Paul's resume of inflictions.

What anyone else dares to boast about—I am speaking as a fool—I also dare to boast about. Are they Hebrews? So am I. Are they Israelites? So am I. Are they Abraham's descendants? So am I. Are they servants of Christ? (I am out of my mind to talk like this.) I am more. I have worked much harder, been in prison more frequently, been flogged more severely, and been exposed to death again and again. Five times I received from the Jews the forty lashes minus one. Three times I was beaten with rods, once I was stoned, three times I was shipwrecked, I spent a night and a day in the open sea, I have been constantly on the move. I have been in danger from rivers, in danger from bandits, in danger from my own countrymen, in danger from Gentiles; in danger in the city, in danger in the country, in danger at sea; and in danger from false brothers. I have labored and toiled and have often gone without sleep; I have known hunger and thirst and have often gone without food; I have been cold and naked. Besides everything else, I face daily the pressure of my concern for all the churches. Who is weak, and I do not feel weak? Who is led into sin, and I do not inwardly burn?

13) **What do you think Paul is saying in this passage?**

_____

_____

_____

14) **Remember when Christ changed your life. What immediate impact did it have?**

_____

_____

_____

15) **What changed about you once you accepted Christ?**

_____

_____

_____

The Edge
John 19:11 *"You would have no power over me if it were not given to you from above."*

To win in this life we have to define the word "win". Winning in life cannot be measured by any of the world's standards. The measuring stick must be defined by our attitudes, attempts, perseverance, and cause.

16) **How would you define winning?**

_____

_____

_____

17) **Does the thought of winning with a Christ-like view seem strange to you?**

_____

_____

_____

My sister was diagnosed with Lymphomas many years a go. The doctors gave her six months to live. My sister is a wonderful Christian woman whom I respect very much. At the time of her diagnosis she had three wonderful little children.

My sister made a decision, which has impacted my life tremendously: to win over this life and the standards this world sets for us. With God's guidance she is still with us to this day and has raised those three wonderful children. She lost her youngest to a cyst on the brain when my niece was only seventeen. The courage, love, and perseverance my sister has shown has made her an all-time hero in my life. She understands how life can be cruel but she has the edge that continues to raise her above what this world will throw at her. When I get the opportunity to get together with her I always leave her presence feeling better than when I arrived. She chose to win and that attitude is contagious.

18) Are you ready to live life to the fullest?

_____

_____

_____

19) Will you be willing to accept a better rewards system?

_____

_____

_____

20) Can you accept that the world has been telling you a lie?

_____

_____

_____

Study Guide:
To Win-Build-and Send
Preparing to Live a Truly Great
Life in Christ
(Ch. 2)

—៣៣—

Why Win
Luke 19:10*"For the Son of Man came to seek and to save what was lost."*

I used to coach Jr. High sports at a private school in Houston, TX... I always quoted to my teams **1 Peter 4:11** *"If anyone speaks, he should do it as one speaking the very words of God. If anyone serves, he should do it with the strength God provides, so that in **all things** God may be praised through Jesus Christ. To him be the glory and the power for ever and ever. Amen."*

1)   **What does this passage say to you?**

_____
_____
_____

Being Consistent
Malachi 3:6 *"I the LORD do not change."*

2) **What is your perception upon the Lord never changing? What do you base your thoughts upon?**

_____

_____

_____

We tend to separate areas of our life and how we can react and handle those areas. We may react to our friends in a much different attitude than we would a family member. We may put on a separate face for an employee versus our employer. We may refrain from showing out temper in public but explode behind the doors of our home.

2) **Can you reflect upon a time when you had a "double-standard" in the way you react with different people? (Do you treat different people different ways?)**

_____

_____

_____

To win in life we must be consistent in how we live this life in all circumstances.

3) **What does "consistency" in behavior look like to you?**

_____

_____

_____

Offering consistency to those around us brings stability to everyone's life. Most of our traits are learned behaviors. A learned behavior is a particular way we act, respond, or handle life. Do we communicate well? If not then it is probably a product of how we observed others communicate throughout our lives. Do we handle conflict well? If not then we probably didn't have good role models in those areas.

5) What type of role models did you encounter that may have shaped the way you react to situations in life?

_____

_____

_____

How to "Win"
1 Corinthians 9:19 *"Though I am free and belong to no man, I make myself a slave to everyone, to win as many as possible."*

To understand what we are winning we have to understand how to win.

6) How do you define "how to win"?

_____

_____

_____

The Bible tells us that *"For the message of the cross is foolishness to those who are perishing, but to us who are being saved it is the power of God."* (1 Corinthians 1:18)

7) What does this verse say to you?

_____

_____

_____

I believe the answer to the "how" question is to live life in a way that others cannot refute that the Holy Living God dwells in you. Live a life where God directs your attitudes. Be willing to share the gospel when the occasion presents itself. Be willing to preach without speaking because the Light of the World is shining through you.

8)   What does "sharing the Gospel" look like to you?

_____

_____

_____

Winning the Believer

Galatians 3:22 *"But the Scripture declares that the whole world is a prisoner of sin, so that what was promised, being given through faith in Jesus Christ, might be given to those who believe."*

9)   Have you looked at yourself as being a prisoner to sin?

_____

_____

_____

When you understand that God is up to something in every situation, and that He is in control, and that you cannot lose no matter the circumstance then we start to affect everyone and everything around us.

10)   Am I allowing God to have total control over every situation in my life?

_____

_____

_____

11) Do I handle my trials myself first or do I go to God
    and trust Him with my trials first?

    _____

    _____

    _____

12) Am I willing to give up control of my life to God?

    _____

    _____

    _____

Study Guide:
To Win-Build-and Send
Preparing to Live a Truly Great
Life in Christ
(Ch. 3)

—ᴧᴧ—

How do I Win Inwardly?

Romans 12:2 *"Do not conform to the pattern of this world, but be transformed by the renewing of your mind. Then you will be able to test and approve what God's will is—his good, pleasing and perfect will."*

1)   **When you think of the word "conform" what does it mean to you?**

_____

_____

_____

Can a Person Change?

Romans 12:2 *"Do not conform any longer to the pattern of this world, but be transformed by the renewing of your mind. Then you will be able to test and approve what God's will is—his good, pleasing and perfect will."*

2)   **Is it possible for people to change their lifestyle upon their own?**

_____

_____

_____

3)   **What is needed to make a permanent change in a person's life?**

_____

_____

_____

Philippians 4:13 tells us, *"I can do everything through him who gives me strength."*

4)   **Is this scripture relevant in your life? Why or Why not?**

_____

_____

_____

Being Empowered

Acts 1:8 *"But you will receive power when the Holy Spirit comes on you..."*

5) **Have you ever had a moment when you felt above average strength spiritually, emotionally, or physically?**

_____

_____

_____

You can win inwardly when you stop seeing yourself as the world dictates; fame, power, money, popularity, etc, and you start seeing yourself for what you are becoming in Christ. You cannot be effective for the long term outwardly until you allow God to have the victory over the inwardly.

6) **What does "winning inwardly" describe to you?**

_____

_____

_____

7) **Have you allowed God to have victory over all of your life?**

_____

_____

_____

Romans 8:37, *"No, in all these things we are more than conquerors through him who loved us."* You have been empowered with a power that the world cannot defeat. You have been set a part for a perfect work.

8) **Do you gauge yourself by the standards of the world or by the understanding of what God is making you into?**

_____

_____

_____

9) **Can you accept that you have been empowered by the Holy Spirit to carry out the service that God has called you to?**

_____

_____

_____

Take a moment and really think about this question. How we actually gauge our lives is very important. Pray that you may see yourself as God sees you

Study Guide:
To Win-Build-and Send
Preparing to Live a Truly Great
Life in Christ
(Ch. 4)

—⚏—

The How of Outwardly Winning

1 Timothy 4:8 *"For physical training is of some value, but godliness has value for all things, holding promise for both the present life and the life to come."*

1)   **What is godliness?**

_____

_____

_____

2)   **What does the term *"for all things"* refer to in this passage?**

_____

_____

_____

3)   **What are the promises referred to in this passage?**

_____

_____

_____

Fellowship

1 John 1:7 *"But if we walk in the light, as he is in the light, we have fellowship with one another, and the blood of Jesus, his Son, purifies us from all sin."*

4)   **Explain the "how" of fellowship contained in this passage.**

_____

_____

_____

I believe there are three things a believer needs to be involved in to prepare themselves for outwardly winning. The first is being a part of a healthy, encouraging fellowship of believers.

5)   **What does a healthy, encouraging fellowship of believers look like to you?**

_____

_____

_____

6)   **Are you a contributing part of that fellowship?**

_____

_____

_____

Winning through Growing

2 Corinthians 10:15 *"Neither do we go beyond our limits by boasting of work done by others. Our hope is that, as your faith continues to grow, our area of activity among you will greatly expand"*

The second suggestion I would have is to go deeper. To truly win outwardly we must learn the Word and know how to apply it. Without a Bible study, small group, Sunday school, or some type of more-in-depth study we cannot be properly prepared to live out the victory.

7) **Do you believe the above statement to be true for spiritual growth and maturity?**

_____

_____

_____

8) **What does *"going deeper"* look like to you?**

_____

_____

_____

Paul, when the scales were removed from his eyes, sat under the teaching of the apostles. In Acts chapter two we read that the believers sat under the teaching of the apostles. We need to be taught the Word and we need to have a firm understanding of the Word.

9) **Why is it so hard for us to discipline ourselves to a constant study of the Word?**

_____

_____

_____

10) **Is a firm understanding of the Word important? Why or why not?**

_____

_____

_____

Getting into the Game

1 Peter 4:13 *"But rejoice that you participate in the sufferings of Christ, so that you may be overjoyed when his glory is revealed."*

The third aspect of wining outwardly is to discover your spiritual gifts and put them to use.

11) **How can we** *"participate in the sufferings of Christ"*?

_____

_____

_____

12) **How could doing this bring joy to our lives?**

_____

_____

_____

There are wonderful tools to help you discover your gifts. I encourage you to truly seek out your gifts but also remember knowledge is not enough. One of the best ways to win outwardly is for others to see you working in your gifts. When people work in their gifts they work in an area of passion. They enjoy what they are doing and that is contagious.

13) **Have you discovered your spiritual gifts?**

_____

_____

_____

14) **Are you using those gifts?**

_____

_____

_____

15) Have you seen someone else blessed by your gifts?

_____

_____

_____

16) Why, when we use our gifts, do those gifts bring such joy to us and others?

_____

_____

_____

When I was in a church in Akron, Ohio, there was a little old lady who watered the plants every Sunday. She brought two milk jugs full of water every Sunday and placed them under her pew. After the service she would march around the church singing children's songs and would water the plants. I noticed that after some time the kids started following her. They would follow her singing those songs and helping her water the plants. These kids were enjoying her gifts and at the same time learning about Christ. I cannot tell you how many adults were blessed by the sight of this as well.

17) Have I allowed God to win me inwardly?

_____

_____

_____

18) Have I trusted Him with my whole life?

_____

_____

_____

19) Am I allowing God to use me to win my family members?

_____

_____

_____

20) Do I trust in Him to win those around me in my life?

_____

_____

_____

21) What must I do in my life to allow God to lead me to win others to him?

_____

_____

_____

Study Guide:
To Win-Build-and Send
Preparing to Live a Truly Great
Life in Christ
(Ch. 5)

—ᴍ—

Who Are We to Win?
Matthew 16:25 *"For whoever wants to save their life will lose it, but whoever loses their life for me will find it."*

1)   Can you think of one lost person whom you know?

_____

_____

_____

Who are we to win? That is a question we all must face. In the last chapter we spoke about why we win family, friends, and others. I want to talk about who we are to win in this chapter.

The Lost
Luke 19:10 *"For the Son of Man came to seek and to save what was lost."*

2)   What does *"seek the lost"* mean to you?

_____

_____

_____

The lost are those who have not made Jesus the Lord and Savior of their life. It sounds broad but you can decipher who these people may be.

3) How can we determine who is lost and who is not?

_____

_____

_____

Know your story. Your story is what people really want to hear. They want to know what God has done in your life and why you believe. People will want to know that this is not just a thought but that it actually happened to you. Be prepared to give your story of what God has done in your own life.

4) Do you know your story?

_____

_____

_____

5) Could you tell your story to someone else?

_____

_____

_____

6) Take a moment and think about your story and how you could tell it. If you find this difficult maybe you could write down your story for practice.

_____

_____

_____

Pray for the person who is lost. When we pray for people specifically we seem to grow in affection for the person being prayed for. Pray for them everyday. Pray for God to open opportunities to show them the way to Christ. Pray that they will accept the message of the cross. Pray that you will be willing to walk through the door that God opens.

7) **Remember that lost person you thought in question #1? Take a moment right now and pray for that person.**

_____

_____

_____

Winning Strangers

Job 29:16 "*I was a father to the needy; I took up the case of the stranger.*"

8) **What are you doing to bring Christ to those you do not know?**

_____

_____

_____

Well, if you are a believer you have made that choice. Peter tells us in 1 Peter 2:9 "*But you are a chosen people, a **royal priesthood**, a holy nation, a people belonging to God, that you may declare the praises of him who called you out of darkness into his wonderful light.*" Every one of us who has decided to follow Jesus has become a "royal priesthood".

We have been set apart to do His will for it is He that has brought us out of the destructive life we were living. We must live a life that reflects what He has done. Others are watching you, I do not care if you think you are popular or not, there is someone watching you.

9) **Have you ever thought that there is someone who thinks your life is important?**

_____

_____

_____

10) **Have you ever considered your self as "*priesthood*"?**

_____

_____

_____

Winning the Believer
John 13:15 "*I have set you an example that you should do as I have done for you.*"

11) **How can we set examples for those who already know Christ as their Savior?**

_____

_____

_____

I want to encourage you to motivate, encourage, direct, lead, assist, and whatever else it may take to get that person to engage into the game.

12) **Do I exhibit a life to lead others to Christ?**

_____

_____

_____

13) **Am I aware of the lost in my life?**

_____

_____

_____

14) **Am I conscience that others are watching my example?**

_____

_____

_____

Study Guide:
To Win-Build-and Send
Preparing to Live a Truly Great
Life in Christ
(Ch. 6)

—⚡—

What Are We to Win?
Luke 21:19 *"Stand firm, and you will win life."*

Every game that is played, every deal that is won, every fight that is fought has a goal. To win! We are a society that is taught to win. To be taught to win is not a bad thought but at what cost is the true question. We sometimes lose sight of the prize of winning. We seem to be willing to compromise our values, ethics, morals and our time to simply win. By winning this way we forget what it is we are truly trying to win.

Christ said, "I came to serve, not be served." When we start to see others as the object of our service then we start to see them through the eyes of the Almighty Creator of the Universe. Every business, sports team, non-profit agency, government agency and each individual has a goal to pursue. Our goal as living a life that is excellent has many different goals and each goal is from a different view than the world has.

1) **What does *"winning"* mean to you?**

_____

_____

_____

The Goal of Self
Ephesians 4:22 *"You were taught, with regard to your former way of life, to put off your old self, which is being corrupted by its deceitful desires"*

The first goal we will discuss is the goal of self. The goal of self is *"pressing on toward the prize"* as Paul states. We have to realize that this world is not our goal. This world only has temporal prizes to offer us. Yes, it is true; we can leave a legacy to those left behind. We can leave a legacy of what the world can give us; things such as fame, possessions, power, money, and lust, physical pleasure, and etc. What we physically leave behind is a temporary fix. We will pass on from this world and then what?

2) **What would you want to most be remembered for?**

_____

_____

_____

The Goal for Others
Mark 4:20 *"Others, like seed sown on good soil, hear the word, accept it, and produce a crop—thirty, sixty or even a hundred times what was sown."*

3) **What does evangelizing look like to you?**

_____

_____

_____

I cannot tell you how many people, who will never attend the local Sunday sermon that you will have an opportunity to lead to Christ. There are people that simply observe your life without ever interacting. Watch for those people and listen to the prompting of the Holy Spirit. Act upon those leadings.

4) Have you ever been prompted by the Holy Spirit to speak or interact with a stranger?

_____

_____

_____

5) How did you respond to that prompting?

_____

_____

_____

The next group that we should look to win, and not in any order, is those we do know. The family unit is unlike any other relationship out there. We seem to be able to hurt, love, encourage, tear-down and sometimes even despise those in our own families. Yet, with all of that we still can remain in love with those members of our family. I have found that the hardest thing for a family to do is to relay God's love in their own homes. Whatever the reason, we hold back and refrain and sometimes even hope the church will do this job for us.

6) Do you find it difficult to witness to family members?

_____

_____

_____

7)   Do you have a structured family time in the Word?

_____

_____

_____

8)   Would you consider a plan to witness to family members if you do not have one already?

_____

_____

_____

You never know the impact of who you can win and encourage when you live a life that gives every opportunity to those around you to see how Christ is shining through you. We can allow them to see how Christ is changing each of us and how He is helping you to win this game of life.

Take a moment and reflect on the impact you may have on others.

9)   Do they know you are a Christian at your work by the way you interact with others?

_____

_____

_____

10)   Would they know you are a Christian in your community?

_____

_____

_____

I want to encourage you t be aware of the lost in your life. The lost come in and out of it everyday. Pray that the Lord will open your eyes to the opportunities of the lost in your life.

Study Guide:
To Win-Build-and Send
Preparing to Live a Truly Great
Life in Christ
(Ch. 7)

—∿—

Build

Matthew 28:20a *"teaching them to obey everything I have commanded you"*

1)   **What do the words *"obey"* and *"command"* convey to you?**

_____

_____

_____

1 Peter 2:6 *"See, I lay a stone in Zion, a chosen and precious cornerstone, and the one who trust in him will never be put to shame."*

The cornerstone, I have learned, is the most important piece of a building. The weight of the building rests upon the cornerstone. If the cornerstone is weak the whole building will have problems. We must acknowledge that we have to build upon the work Christ has done in us through salvation.

2) **When you lay your burdens upon Christ in prayer do you leave them with Him or pick them back up and take them with you?**

_____

_____

_____

The Concept to Build

Luke 14:28 *"Suppose one of you wants to build a tower. Will he not first sit down and estimate the cost to see if he has enough money to complete it?"*

3) **What would sitting down and really counting the cost look like in your life?**

_____

_____

_____

Preparing to Build

Mark 1:3 *"a voice of one calling in the desert, 'Prepare the way for the Lord, make straight paths for him.'"*

Let me remind you that life is not going to take it easy on you just because you are a Christian. If anything, life will be a little harder on you because you believe in the truth of Christ. This world has Satan running loose upon it. Satan is the *"prince of this world"* according to John 12:31. We should not be surprised that this world is full of deceit and lies.

4) **What is your understanding that Satan is the prince of this world?**

_____

_____

_____

To combat this world we need to be prepared. We can not get by with luck. My high school soccer coach, Alan Baker, had a wonderful saying about luck. He said, "Luck is simply preparation meeting opportunity." I do not personally believe in luck. I believe in divine intervention and I believe that we need to be as prepared as we can for every endeavor as we possibly can be.

5) List some ways you can prepare for the expected and unexpected events in life.

_____

_____

_____

The Bible tells us that we must *"continue to work out your salvation with fear and trembling"* (Philippians 2:12). We should understand from this that it is an on going process. This should also remind us that the road will not always be easy. As we look at this scripture it should make us look at our lives and see if we are "working out our salvation".

6) How does *"working out our salvation"* exhibit itself in our lives?

_____

_____

_____

Breaking Ground
Job 21:33 *"The soil in the valley is sweet to him; all men follow after him, and a countless throng goes before him."*

Each of us, once we have accepted Christ, should step back and take a good look at our lives.
We need to build the gifts and talents and passions we have. We also have to build others. None of the building

that needs to take place can take place if we are not willing to grow.

Take a look at where you are.

7) Are you willing to grow in your relationship with Christ?

_____

_____

_____

8) Are you willing to do the work necessary to "work out your salvation"?

_____

_____

_____

9) Can you take the time to become what He is calling you to be?

_____

_____

_____

If the answer is yes, I want to encourage you. You are about to go on a ride that will, not can, change your life forever. Now hang on because, here we go!

Study Guide:
To Win-Build-and Send
Preparing to Live a Truly Great
Life in Christ
(Ch. 8)

—⟶⟶—

The Foundation

Matthew 7:24 *"Therefore everyone who hears these words of mine and puts them into practice is like a wise man who built his house on the rock."*

1)　**What does it entail to put the words of the Bible into practice?**

_____

_____

_____

The foundation is the most crucial element of living a truly great life in Christ. We must first grasp that God is in control and can be fully trusted. Many Christians say this but very few practice it. To practice this it means we have to understand that no matter how great or how horrific the situation may seem that we are okay because God has already worked it all out.

We need to get to the place that we are not controlled by our emotions, but trust in a sovereign Lord totally. Then, and only then, we can see life in a light that exposes the world's weakness and acknowledges the strength of God in all circumstances. The light of Christ will expose all truths.

2)   List some ways we can practice trusting the Lord in all circumstances.

_____

_____

_____

3)   How do we look for God in all circumstances and events in our lives?

_____

_____

_____

Emotions

Titus 2:12 *"It teaches us to say "No" to ungodliness and worldly passions, and to live self-controlled, upright and godly lives in this present age,"*

4)   What does the word self-controlled look like to you in everyday life?

_____

_____

_____

When trials come into our life we must not react on emotions. We must react after we reflect upon our training.

5)   What part do emotions play in your decision making procedure?

_____

_____

_____

To really live a great life in Christ we must first be willing to build a foundation in ourselves that is based upon the Word of God.

6) What does the Word of God have to do with our emotions?

_____

_____

_____

Growing

Deuteronomy 32:2 *"Let my teaching fall like rain*
and my words descend like dew,
like showers on new grass,
like abundant rain on tender plants."

7) What does this verse speak to you?

_____

_____

_____

When a new believer comes to me and asked what they should do, I always direct them to get involved in the three aspects of spiritual growth, fellowship, study, and involvement make-up these three aspects.

8) Do you have a personal involvement in any of the above activities? List those that you are actively involved with.

_____

_____

_____

The Apostle Paul had his foundation torn apart by a personal experience. He was on the road to Damascus when he had a personal experience with Jesus Christ. The moment literally left him blinded. He immediately had to rely on others for everything. This personal experience that blinded him, allowed him to see the true light which was Jesus Christ.

9) **Have you had a personal experience that has brought you closer to God? If so, please list that experience here.**

_____

_____

_____

10) **Are you erratic with your emotions?**

_____

_____

11) **Do others shy away from certain topics because of how you may react?**

_____

_____

_____

12) **Are you growing in your relationship with God?**

_____

_____

_____

13) **Are you growing in your relationships with others?**

_____

_____

_____

Take a moment and reflect on how you may or may not be growing. Make a decision and commit to growing in the good work Christ is doing in you. Stop right now and pray to God and ask Him for guidance and vision in this area of your life.

Study Guide:
To Win-Build-and Send
Preparing to Live a Truly Great
Life in Christ
(Ch. 9)

—⟋⟋⟍—

Building Upward
Genesis 11:9 *"That is why it was called Babel[1]—because there the LORD confused the language of the whole world. From there the LORD scattered them over the face of the whole earth."*

1) **Have you ever had a conversation with a person who did not speak your language? Explain how you communicated.**

   _____
   _____
   _____

Tower of Babel
Proverbs 18:10 *"The name of the LORD is a strong tower; the righteous run to it and are safe."*

In Genesis eleven, we read an interesting story of a people who decided to build. This may sound good in theory. It was a whole community building together, working in harmony, and all for a common good. The problem with this particular community is that they were building for their own glory.

According to verse four, they wanted to build a tower that would reach heaven to make a *"name for themselves"*.

2)   **Have you ever participated in a community event? Describe the event.**

_____

_____

_____

3)   **Have you made a name for yourself in your industry, community, or family? Describe if you can.**

_____

_____

_____

I have taught myself to ask myself a question before every endeavor, response, or action. I ask myself, "How can I bring glory to God with…"

4)   **Do you have a plan to bring God the glory in all circumstances? Describe that plan.**

_____

_____

_____

We must continually build upwards towards God. We must bring Him honor in our whole life. Our life at the moment as well as our long term plans must bring the attention and honor to Christ.

5)   **What would this application resemble in your life?**

_____

_____

_____

From Milk to Solid Food

Hebrews 5:14 *"But solid food is for the mature, who by constant use have trained themselves to distinguish good from evil."*

6) **Have you grown in Christ since the day you accepted Him as your Savior? Explain.**

_____

_____

_____

So many of us come to the Lord and never grow up in Christ. **Hebrews 5:13** tells us, *"Anyone who lives on milk, being still an infant, is not acquainted with the teaching about righteousness."* We need to move from the moment of salvation and start preparing ourselves to be a servant of Christ.

7) **What does a "plan of maturity" resemble in your own life at the present time?**

_____

_____

_____

Christ Himself told us, *"just as the Son of Man did not come to be served, but to serve, and to give his life as a ransom for many."*(Matthew 20:28) So we are made for service as well.

8) **Do you serve your fellow man?**

_____

_____

_____

9) **How can serving others build up our own faith in Christ?**

_____

_____

_____

I want you to consider where you are at in your spiritual maturity. I am going to list a few "benchmarks" for you to consider:

10) **Do you spend daily time in God's Word?**

_____

_____

_____

11) **Do you spend daily time in prayer with God?**

_____

_____

_____

12) **Do you serve God and man?**

_____

_____

_____

13) **Do you desire to grow up in Christ?**

_____

_____

_____

Take a moment and ponder upon these very simple questions. As you review and think upon these questions, ask God to reveal to you where you are not growing and ask Him for guidance and passion in these areas. I also want to remind you that I am praying for you and for your success to truly live a great life in Christ.

Study Guide:
To Win-Build-and Send
Preparing to Live a Truly Great
Life in Christ
(Ch. 10)

—ᘯ—

Building Others
Ephesians 4:12 *"to equip his people for works of service, so that the body of Christ may be built up"*

1)   **How does this verse speak to you personally?**

_____
_____
_____

   I referred, in the book, a story about how my high school soccer built me up physically and emotionally, have you ever invested your time into someone else's life? Explain.

Being a Coach
Psalm 199:35 *"Direct me in the path of your commands, for there I find delight."*

2)   **What directions to you truly follow in life?**

_____
_____
_____

Coaching is not about knowing the answers. No, coaching someone is helping them find the answers. Coaching knows where to send others for the answers.

3) **Where do you send people for advice when asked? Where do you get your information to give advice from?**

_____

_____

_____

The art of mentoring is almost a lost practice in the Christian community today.

4) **What keeps us from taking people to mentor?**

_____

_____

_____

5) **How would you approach someone to become a mentor to them?**

_____

_____

_____

Being a Friend
John 15:13 *"Greater love has no one than this, that he lay down his life for his friends."*

6) **Do you have a friend, non-relative, whom you would lay your life down for?**

_____

_____

_____

We need to be willing to risk pleasing people and allow the friendship to exhibit the love of the truth in their lives. The Bible is very clear that our *"yes be yes, and our no be no."* We cannot build people's faith by being unclear with the gospel.

7) **How can we present the Gospel to others through relationship building?**

_____

_____

_____

Husbands and Wives

1 Corinthians 7:16 *"How do you know, wife, whether you will save your husband? Or, how do you know, husband, whether you will save your wife?"*

I want to take a moment and speak to those of you who are married or will be one day. I have found one of the best ways to build up my partner is to do two very simple things. I have found that by praying out loud with my wife, we have opened a whole new dimension in our communication.

8) **Why do you think that "praying out loud" with my spouse has helped us to communicate?**

_____

_____

_____

9) **How does communicating well with my spouse allow me to communicate well with others?**

_____

_____

_____

The second thing Cami and I do to build each other in Christ is to read together. Whether we are reading the Bible, a devotional, or a book together we have found that to read aloud and share with each other allows us to learn better, understand each others passions more, and it lays a foundation for communication.

10) How does reading God's Word allow us to build each other up in Christ?

_____

_____

_____

Christ knows what each of us needs in order to grow. If we say yes to the opportunities He presents for us, He will grow us. Listen to Him and be willing to step out into new territories. I want to have you think for just a moment about how you are building the people in your lives:

11) Are you reaching out to them with the truth?

_____

_____

_____

12) Are you willing to mentor them?

_____

_____

_____

13) Are you willing to risk your comfort zones and step out into the unknown with them and Christ?

_____

_____

_____

Take a moment and pray about these issues and ask Christ to give you the understanding and courage to do His will.

Study Guide:
To Win-Build-and Send
Preparing to Live a Truly Great
Life in Christ
(Ch. 11)

—⚏—

Send
Matthew 28:19a *"Therefore go"*

1) **What do you think of when you think of the word "go"?**

_____

_____

_____

Sending Yourself
Acts 22:21 *"Then the Lord said to me, 'Go; I will send you far away to the Gentiles.'"*

2) **Do you believe that every Christian is being sent to spread the Word of God?**

_____

_____

_____

To be willing simply means you have to trust in the One who called you. When Jesus walked this earth just his presence must have had a profound effect upon people. We can read the stories of how they left everything to follow Him. They left their jobs, homes, families, money, and material possessions to simply follow a man that they just met.

3) Have you ever felt God calling you to something? How did you react?

_____

_____

_____

To be sent out we have to be willing to go.

4) Are you willing to answer a call from God that you are uncomfortable with? Explain.

_____

_____

_____

Sending out Others
2 Corinthians 13:13 *"All the saints send their greetings."*

5) Is it difficult to consider yourself a saint?

_____

_____

_____

Missionaries, pastors, teachers, leaders, elders, deacons, and many other positions in the church seem to be what I thought of when I thought about people being sent out to do the Lord's work. I never seemed to think of mothers, fathers, doctors, firemen, police officers, friends, janitors, and the rest of the people I run into on a daily basis.

6) **Who do you think about when you think of someone being sent out to do ministry?**

_____

_____

_____

Every believer that comes into our lives has been given a gift by God. Most of these individuals have been given more than one gift.

7) **Have you seen someone working in their giftedness? What did it look like?**

_____

_____

_____

If we truly want to build the Kingdom of Christ we need to allow people to be truly all that God has designed them to be.

8) **What does un-conventional ministry look like to you? Would you support ministry that is uncommon?**

_____

_____

_____

9) **Can you encourage a person in a ministry that you personally would not be involved with?**

_____

_____

_____

If we truly want to build the Kingdom of Christ we need to allow people to be truly all that God has designed them to be.

10) **Can you list a gift or gifts that you may see in yourself?**

_____

_____

_____

11) **Can you list gifts that you have seen in others?**

_____

_____

_____

There are many different stages to a physical life. To name a few, there is infancy, toddler, child, adolescent, young adult, adult, middle age, and the senior adult. Many stages of the physical life exhibit many different stages of physical abilities. I may go from crawling to walking, from walking to running, and from running to simply walking again. As I mature physically my body allows me to do things differently.

12) **How does the physical growth in life relate to the spiritual growth we may encounter in our Christian life?**

_____

_____

_____

Think about what God is doing around you and how you can be involved. Think about the gifts, passions and abilities He has granted you and how these things can be used to build His Kingdom. What is He really putting upon your heart? Understand it may be for the time as it is now or it may be building you for a later time in your life.

Take just a moment to understand your gifts more. I want to encourage you to ask yourself a couple of questions:

13) **Do you trust God with the gifts that He has given you?**

_____

_____

_____

14) **Are you willing to step out of your comfort zone and serve Him with your gifts?**

_____

_____

_____

15) **Is there someone you can encourage in their gifts and passions?**

_____

_____

_____

16) **Am I open to the fact that God can use me for such a time as this?**

_____

_____

_____

17) **Am I willing to be used for what God wants in the lives of others?**

_____

_____

_____

Take a moment and pray how God can better use you to encourage others in your life. Remember, I am praying for you as well.

Study Guide:
To Win-Build-and Send
Preparing to Live a Truly Great
Life in Christ
(Ch. 12)

—⟁—

Your Gifts for Others
1 Peter 4:10 '*Each of you should use whatever **gift** you have received to serve others, as faithful stewards of God's grace in its various forms.*"

1.   **What does serving others look like to you?**

   _____

   _____

   _____

2.   **Do you currently serve in a position where you serve others? At your church, work, community, or home?**

   _____

   _____

   _____

   Serving others is not a popular statement to be made in our self-serving society. America is a society that wants to be served. We have drive-thru fast food, drive-thru banks, and we even have drive-thru wedding chapels. We have people who can do our nails, hair, face, and feet. We want to be served and we want it now! We look at somebody serving us as someone beneath us.

3. **Have you ever found yourself treating someone as less than yourself because of their position or circumstance? Explain.**

    _____

    _____

    _____

Jesus was the most gifted teacher this world has or will ever see. He was superior in His knowledge. He was advanced in His ability to speak. He was able to control His tongue when others could not. He had a following that would make any power seeker envious. Yet, we read in John thirteen that Jesus became the servant to teach a lesson. He took on the role of the lowest servant to wash each of the disciples' feet.

4. **Think of the lowest position of service in your mind, can you see yourself serving others in this position? Why or why not?**

    _____

    _____

    _____

Our churches today need people to be willing to serve in their gifts. We need to reach out to the hurting and lost. It seems that so many churches leave all of the service to the minister or to the few who do volunteer. When we can see that every believer has a gift to offer to others, and encourage them to serve others, we will be totally shocked at what the church can do.

5. **Can you think of an area of service that you could use your gifts in your church?**

    _____

    _____

    _____

6. **Has the Lord impressed upon your heart an area of service He is urging you to get involved with?**

    _____

    _____

    _____

If you see any area where you need to engage your gifts for the benefit of others I want you to ask God to lead you right now in that knowledge. Ask His Holy Spirit to guide you down the path to impart your gifts on others. This may be done through a program at your church or it may be an individual effort. Whatever it may be, do not allow the joy of service, in your gifts, pass you by.

I encourage you to really seek the answers to the following questions:

7. **Can you see yourself as a servant to those you look down upon?**

    _____

    _____

    _____

8. **Will you seek out someone to bless with your gifts?**

    _____

    _____

    _____

9. **Can you serve someone and not seek out gratitude for your service?**

_____

_____

_____

You may not receive the recognition, fame, or headlines for serving others upon this earth but know, *"And without faith it is impossible to please God, because anyone who comes to him must believe that he exists and that he **rewards** those who earnestly seek him."* (Hebrews 11:6)

Study Guide:
To Win-Build-and Send
Preparing to Live a Truly Great
Life in Christ
(Ch. 13)

—m—

Encouragement for You and Others
Matthew 28:20 *"surely I am with you always"*

1) **What does *"surely I am with you always"* say to you?**

_____

_____

_____

Life is going to throw you twist and fears whenever it can. The one great encouragement is that God is always with us. No matter what is going on He will never leave us alone. He has made this a promise... We do go through times when we are in the valley and the valley is a very lonely place for us to be.

We were made for relationship and, when the one relationship that gave us the very heart that beats in us seems so far away, we can become very lonely. Jesus understood this all to well. When Christ was upon the cross he asked this question of God, *About three in the afternoon Jesus cried out in a loud voice, "Eli, Eli, lema sabachthani?" (which means "My God, my God, why have you forsaken me?").*(Matthew

27:46) For just a moment the pain, anguish, sadness and still-ness of the cross had Jesus in the valley. For just that moment he felt all alone. The people of the earth had rejected Him, the disciples had fled from Him, and His Father seemed so far away.

2) **Have you ever felt that you were alone and that God had abandoned you? Explain.**

_____

_____

_____

3) **Have you ever been in a spiritual valley? Explain.**

_____

_____

_____

4) **What does the verse *"My God, my God, why have you forsaken me?"* say to you?**

_____

_____

_____

God is always with us and, whether we feel him or not, He is still there. We have to come to a point of trust in Christ that no matter how we feel or how big the circumstance we are not alone.

5) **Does this seem like a difficult understanding to you? Explain.**

_____

_____

_____

God has a way that we cannot understand but, when we look back, we can see the hand of God and where it has been in our lives.

6) **Can you look back on a time in your life and see where God was working? Write about that time.**

_____

_____

_____

I want to remind you that the battle is not fought in the valley. Moses, in the Bible, was standing on the mountain as the Israelites fought a battle. He remained on the mountain with his arms lifted to heaven. As his hands would lower the Israelites would begin to lose the battle. When his hands went towards heaven the Israelites would begin to win the battle. The battle was being fought in the spiritual realms and not in the physical valley. Our battles are not fought in the valley either. No, our battles are being fought in the spiritual realms as well.

7) **Is there comfort in knowing that the battles in life are being fought in the spiritual realms?**

_____

_____

_____

—ᗰ—

No matter what the mountain is that comes your way, you have the Holy Spirit with you every step of the way. When we accept Christ we are given the Holy Spirit as a comforter. This comforter is with us and we have a source of strength that the world does not have. The world cannot conquer the Spirit and the world does not have the means or knowledge to defeat our God. Trust in the Lord and know that He is there and that He will never leave you.

Points of encouragement:

- **Know that God is always there.**

- **Know that you can never separate yourself from Gods love. (Romans 8:39)**

- **You are special.**

- **You were designed for success.**

- **You have been prayed for.**

Take a moment and just thank the Lord for being there. Thank Him for being there when you did not feel Him or see Him. I want to encourage you, just as I saw with the people of The Hospitality House, to look for God to show up when all seems lost. He will not let you down.

Study Guide:
To Win-Build-and Send
Preparing to Live a Truly Great
Life in Christ
(Closing Thoughts)

—ɯɯ—

Win-Build-Send for the Kingdom of Christ
(May you live a truly great life in Christ)
(Ch. 14)
John 10:10b *"I have come that they may have life, and have it to the full."*

I want to thank you for taking the time to read this book. I pray that you have been encouraged to *Win- Build- and Send for the Kingdom of Christ.* It is not enough to read this book and then set it aside. It is not enough to know what you should do but to never do it. It is not enough to get a gift and never open it.

1. **Are you ready to live life to the full?**

_____

_____

_____

I want you to take what you have learned and use it in your families, local church, community, work place and every-where you may travel. Let people see that you have been won from the world by Christ. Allow yourself to encourage

191

others to come to know Christ as their Savior. Be excited to grow in your faith and to become all you can become in Christ. Employ joy so that you may also invest into other lives that you may come into contact with.

2. **Name some areas that you are ready to apply the Win, Build, and Send method.**

———————————————————————

———————————————————————

———————————————————————

3. **Take a moment and ask God to lead you in those areas and to give you a clear vision for His plans for you.**

Allow yourself to be sent into the areas of life to minister to those God is directing you to. Look for opportunities to send others on their way in Christ. Encourage them in their gifts and passions. Encourage them to step-out in faith. Encourage them to become servants to God and man.

Together we can change the world but it starts one life at a time. It starts with a willing life. It starts with a life that will glorify God in all things. It starts with you.

———————————————————————

———————————————————————

———————————————————————

Printed in the United States
69896LV00002B/187-225